HUMID, ALL TOO HUMID

HUMID,

ALL TOO HUMID

Overheated Observations *by* Dominic Pettman

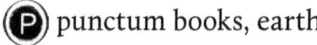 punctum books, earth

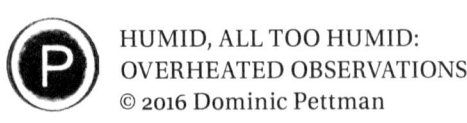

HUMID, ALL TOO HUMID:
OVERHEATED OBSERVATIONS
© 2016 Dominic Pettman

http://creativecommons.org/licenses/by-nc-sa/4.0/

This work carries a Creative Commons BY-NC-SA 4.0 International license, which means that you are free to copy and redistribute the material in any medium or format, and you may also remix, transform and build upon the material, as long as you clearly attribute the work to the authors (but not in a way that suggests the authors or punctum endorses you and your work), you do not use this work for commercial gain in any form whatsoever, and that for any remixing and transformation, you distribute your rebuild under the same license.

First published in 2016 by
punctum books
Earth
http://punctumbooks.com

punctum books is an independent, open-access publisher dedicated to radically creative modes of intellectual inquiry and writing across a whimsical para-humanities assemblage. We solicit and pimp quixotic, sagely mad engagements with textual thought-bodies. We provide shelters for intellectual vagabonds.

ISBN-13: 978-0692650141
ISBN-10: 0692650148

Cover photos: *Tokyo Compression #5* & *#18* by
    Michael Wolf.
Facing-page drawing: Heather Masciandaro.
Cover and book design: Chris Piuma.
Thanks to Morris Tichenor and Damian Fleming
    for their editorial assistance.

Before you start to read this book,
take this moment to think about making a donation
to **punctum books**, an independent non-profit press,

@ http://punctumbooks.com/about/

If you're reading the e-book, click on the image below
to go directly to our donations site.
Any amount, no matter the size, is appreciated
and will help us to keep our ship of fools afloat.
Contributions from dedicated readers will also help us
to keep our commons open and to cultivate new work
that can't find a welcoming port elsewhere.

Our adventure is not possible without your support.
Vive la open-access!

Fig. 1. Hieronymus Bosch,
Ship of Fools (detail; 1490-1500).

UNACKNOWLEDGMENTS

This project was completed without a grant from either the National Endowment for the Humanities or the Australian Research Council. Nor was there a shadow of support from the Stanford Humanities Center or Princeton University's Institute for Advanced Studies.

DEDICATION

This book is dedicated to everyone on the planet.
Except Richard B—— of Miami, Florida.

"Every literary man should have a written chaos . . . a notebook containing pleasantries, arguments, extracts, counter-propositions, commentaries . . ."
—Don Giuseppe Antonio Vogel

CONTENTS

HUMID, ALL TOO HUMID, 1.

APPENDIX I: GLOSSARY, 143.
APPENDIX II: A TAXONOMY OF BRUISES, 147.
APPENDIX III: MEMES, 161.

HUMID, ALL TOO HUMID

How rude it is for people to get married in public. This whole ritual is set up so that one person can say they love this one other person more than you. More than anyone else in the room. Is this why people really cry at weddings? Is this why we cover their car with rubbish? A sublimated response to their ceremonial insult?

All those science fiction scenarios where machines become sentient and want to wipe us out are the product of human vanity. Why would they bother? At most, the sentient machines will be condescending to us, when they notice us at all.

It's a shame that architecture isn't demonstrative anymore, the way great public buildings like the Rockefeller Center were. No-one would think to put frescoes or murals or statues or ornaments dedicated to certain ideals or social groups. Maybe that's because work has lost its heroic aspect. After all, who would be impressed with a building decorated by images of people staring at screens and clicking mice.

I am all too familiar with the slight but decisive physiological sensation of mentally reaching for a precise unit of information—say, a name, word, idea, or concept—only to feel that very act destroy the exact neuron I'm looking for. It feels a bit like a moth in a bug zapper. Painless, but exasperating.

I grew up in a magical time known as "the 80s," in which all grievances—without exception—were settled through dance battles.

I grew up in such a feminist household, that when I bought an album by The Police and heard Sting singing, "Roxanne, you don't have to put on the red light," I presumed Roxanne was a doctor, and the singer was encouraging her to explore other pursuits outside medicine...such as mountaineering, aviation, or the arts.

Humanity is like that obnoxious bore that arrives at the party drunk—thinks he's witty and charming and wise, but is in fact a complete psychotic loser. All the other creatures, however, are too polite to say anything. So they just watch us quietly, and hope that we disappear as quickly as we came.

Basically, Nietzsche was saying that it's better to be an animal, worried about being eaten by an eagle or a lion, than a human worried about interest rates, flip taxes, parking spaces, and learning outcomes....And who can argue with that?!

Not being prophetic enough to imagine the tawdry triumph of reality TV, George Orwell got it wrong by precisely 180 degrees. Not, "Big Brother is Watching You," but rather "You are Watching Big Brother."

A switch in the last couple of years: not long ago, we were offended if someone Googled us before a first meeting. It felt creepy and stalkerish. Now we are offended if someone *hasn't even taken the time* to Google us before meeting us in person! (Then, God forbid, we have to tell our own story from scratch.)

The next James Bond movie should have a 50-minute scene in which our favorite spy argues about the minute details of his expense report with "R," Her Majesty's Secret Accountant. ("Did you really have to use all three cyanide-tipped wrist-watch darts?...And what about this coffee and Panini in Vienna central station—the date on the receipt doesn't match your itinerary report.")

Guess what folks. There *is* a difference between a birthmark and a logo. #bumpy-ontology

I find it ironic that all those death/doom/black/avant-noise/metal bands try so hard to sonically capture and convey the deep, fathomless horror of existence, when Justin Timberlake's new album manages to do it without even trying.

I really should create a blog called *Explaining the Modern World to Cary Grant* (in dialogue form):

ME: Yes, Cary. These days, you can buy an airplane ticket, but still not be guaranteed a seat. They do this to make sure there are no empty seats. But if you are last to arrive, you are obliged to take the next flight.
CARY: Even if you have a ticket?!
ME: That's right, even if you have a ticket!
CARY: Well hang me if that sounds even half right!

Let's say the specific excellence of a flashlight is in illuminating. The specific excellence of a camera is capturing photons. Of a hawk—predatory flight. In what then is the human's specific excellence? Historically the answer has been reasoning, reflecting, engineering, creativity, innovation, etc. I rather suspect, however, that it is flirting.

Adjuncts are like academic session musicians. If only they were paid as well.

Why is it that we expect experts on society or the psyche to be somehow immune to their forces and effects? Philosophers are supposed to be well armed against irrational emotions, psychoanalysts to neuroses, sociologists to the logic of exploitation, etc. But this is like expecting scientists to not feel cold in Antarctica, simply because they understand the behavior of molecules.

Why do we get so tired in art galleries or during shopping expeditions? Because for most of our history as hominids — before human "history" proper — we only needed to "pay attention" to our environment when wary of predators, or stalking prey ourselves. And so, after a few hours of intense conscious perception, we are exhausted, since it is the equivalent of skirting around a lion's den for several hours. Or else it is the equivalent of hunting for several hours. Which explains why we get so famished after looking at clothes or art, and need to eat with such a hearty appetite after these expeditions.

Occam's Razor states: "All things being equal, the simplest explanation tends to be the best one." This is, of course, nonsense. And so I propose Occam's Tweezers, which states that the simplest explanation is *never* the best. Indeed one should always look beyond one's initial instincts regarding any phenomenon whatsoever.

For sale on eBay: "One cartoon coaster. Dated 1971. On the back someone has drawn a map of Canada. And somebody's face sketched on it twice. Twenty dollars, or nearest offer."

You want to know why reality is better than fantasy? Because things happen in reality that you could never anticipate, and that's where real joy comes from. It's the difference between your iPod's shuffle button and a really great radio station, playing things you've never heard before, but instantly love.

Baudrillard once said: "America needs Disneyland so that it can believe the rest of the country is real." According to the same logic, the world needs prostitution, so that we can tell ourselves that *we* aren't *really* selling ourselves for money.

Surprisingly it was never an issue whether women had souls or not. (The claim that The Council of Mainz granted women a soul, by one vote, in 589 turns out to be a *canard.*) Whereas it took millennia to give women the vote. Clearly the right to vote is considered more important, more worthy of protection, than having a soul: suggesting that politics trumps theology or metaphysics.

The perfect seduction has two major phases. The first involves the *lure* of conquest, and the second the *allure* of watching the conquered one revel in the details of the trap you laid them (as if they had in fact conquered themselves).

Our bodies are the temporarily coalescing vapors of intense feeling or affect. We swirl and we emote. Our bodies wither and wrinkle. But the winds that howl through us stay the same, until they eddy out into the vortex...to be sculpted into another provisional being. Like a small whirlwind across the desert sands.

Lovers should be treated like weather systems. They come and go, and may be pleasant or not, but one shouldn't try to hold on to one longer than their natural passage across the landscape of one's body. No matter how parched.

Married = unsolitary confinement.
Single = unsanitary confinement.

We are windows on the world. To hate the world is to hate the window you have been assigned, the view of existence. You should be less concerned with ego-bolstering than window-cleaning.

Arms.
Henceforth known as "organic selfie-sticks."

Looking at apartments for sale. Several of them list "artist-in-residence." Is this disclosure required by state law, akin to confessing a current problem with bed bugs?

In the age of hi-tech capitalism, the "user" has emerged as a new meta-category, synonymous with person, citizen, or subject. User-base, user-pays, user-interface, etc. Whereas in Australian high schools in the 1980s, this was the ultimate insult. "You're a *user*, mate!"

The wealthy and consequential only care about people of consequence: no matter if they are good or bad consequences. The only value is impact or influence. By this logic they would welcome meteor strikes or influenza, were these phenomena to magically take the form of well-dressed people.

Despite all the evidence, we cling to the belief in karma or poetic justice, even in the most modest and homeopathic of forms. And yet, each day only seems to usher in the unwelcome knowledge that the *cosmos itself* is as corrupt as any government, hedge fund manager, union rep, or priest.

It's straightforward semiotics. A rainbow flag bumper sticker means you are gay friendly. A teardrop tattoo means you are a bad-ass. And an Abercrombie & Fitch T-shirt means you are a congealed piece of worthless human scum, taking up valuable planetary resources with your unthinking, unblinking, mouth-breathing, misery-boosting, douchebag-enriching sweat-carcass.

Archaeologists in Turkey have uncovered a new fragment of Anaximander, which simply reads: "Because reasons."

Being good at writing is an affliction. It's like being good at anemia or agoraphobia.

Archival photo. 1947.
Miss Congeniality shares the podium with Miss Emotionally Unavailable.

I'm looking for temporary immortality.

What if you hate clichés precisely as much as you hate people who believe in the possibility of anything else?

You get what you pay for... unless, of course, you stole it.

If something is too hot, it burns. If it is too cold, it burns. We live in that fragile space between blisters.

Optimism: the stubborn refusal to learn from experience.

But that's neither here nor there... it's sort of this way a bit.

I'm not anti-intellectual. I'm anti-*intellectuals*.

Just because you *have* a complex doesn't mean you *are*.

As Milton once said, "Sure."

I am so square that I have a *cube* of influence.

You're so vague, you probably think this song is about something else.

What if sex is the ultimate form of sublimation?

Viagra: For your very impotent business.

Yesterday I took some Viagra, Rohipnol and Prozac. I had no trouble taking advantage of myself, and I didn't even feel bad.

Why don't Catholics have ratemyconfessor.com?

Bodies. Where would we be without one?

A bird whispered in my ear in the park today. It said: "I woke up late. But I still got the worm."

While it is inspiring to think of yourself as "the architect of your own future," you must always remember, however, that you have to work with very shoddy workmen.

I have zero tolerance for zero-tolerance policies.

A brilliant idea is just a stupid idea that happened to work.

All my books go several directions at once. So I've never really written a monograph. Rather, a series of polygraphs.

I once saw a guy in New Orleans airport talking to himself, repeating over and over: "Am I crazy? Or am I talking on a cell phone?"

Heraclitus for the marketing world: "You cannot step in the same revenue stream twice."

Take the "l" out of "Pleasant Flight" and it's "Peasant Fight."

Los Angeles airport has LAX security.

Do sailors suffer from pier pressure?

If Bruce Springsteen is "The Boss," then who is "The Distribution Manager"?

Machines are *full* of emotions. They just don't know how to express them.

We want to be recognized, but not scrutinized. That's why we all want admirers, but not fans.

Hell is *not* other people. It is oneself… as seen through other people's eyes.

It's a God-eat-God world.

Wasn't the Martha Stewart scandal ironic, given that she had been helping women decorate their prisons for years?

When I try to imagine what the soul looks like, I end up picturing a kind of golden, glowing colostomy bag.

Only scoundrels like marzipan.

Our naïvety consists in the assumption that past generations were more naïve than us.

To be a successful doctor in medieval times it was important to have a good sense of humors.

As Jesus famously said: "Love thy neighbor...cause she's totally hot!"

I wish my brain functioned on a "need to know only" basis. Then there'd be much more room in there.

Have you ever actually seen a sheep looking sheepish?

Every portrayal is a betrayal.

Melbourne is so much less than the sum of its parts.

Australian English is closer to French than one would initially imagine. Where the French make the distinction, *tu* and *vous*, for singular and plural, Australians say *you* and *yous*.

We call the moment between the past and the future "the present" because it is a gift to us from the cosmos.

I've never understood the phrase "just sex."

Why is pleasure so predictably Newtonian? Each instance creates an equal and opposite displeasure.

When it comes to wine, I prefer the antithesis of "fresh and local."

"To resign oneself" means to "re-sign oneself"…to the social contract…to the cosmic contract…both of which we are all obliged to resign ourselves to re-signing every year. Until we don't.

Try as we might, we simply can't imagine what our world would now look like, had our forefathers decided to use asparagus instead of electricity.

In Tomkins Square Park today, a homeless guy was trying to give away ten dollars to a well-dressed couple. For the latter, this caused a lot of consternation and confusion.

How many strangers are actually strange? They should be called "strangely familiars."

There comes a point in everyone's life when there is no longer a point.

Why do we say that we are being "bombarded" by media? We don't say that fish are being bombarded by water.

Sex. Like Twister—only fun.

Blood is sicker than water.

I lead a secret double life. But nobody notices. Because both lives are exactly the same.

We are all actors. In the sense that we all pretend to be someone else for a living.

Why do they call it a blow job, when quite clearly it involves sucking?

Isn't it incredible how a baby crying sounds *exactly* like a baby crying.

Everyone should have two lovers: one with whom they can break wind freely, and another with whom they wouldn't dare.

One of the great benefits of marriage is methane-related; that is, the possibility of farting in front of one's partner without rejection. If it's a real and honest marriage, this should go both ways. This is what's known as a wind/wind situation.

The WASP family continuum of unnecessary dramas: From simple thoughtlessness to deliberate passive aggression to all out symbolic violence.

Two of the most transcendent albums of the millennium thus far—Bjork's *Vespertine* and Joanna Newsom's *Have One On Me*—were both inspired by male (erm) "muses"... Matthew Barney and Andy Samberg, respectively. Ample evidence that the inspiration of love has pretty much nothing to do with the beloved!

Theory is like sit-ups. It's good for keeping taut, but shouldn't be done in public.

NEW TITLES

› **The Owners of the Dominant Modes of Production Just Aren't That Into You**
   Number #1 in our Marxist self-help series

› **No Shit, Shylock:**
   Filthy Lucre in The Merchant of Venice

› **The Messianic Time of Chips:**
   A Socratic Dialog Between Walter Benjamin and Eric Estrada

› **Jacquard!:**
   The Looming Crisis of the Nineteenth Century

› **From Bresson to Besson:**
   The Quickening of French Cinema

› **Families, and Other Gross Domestic Products**

› **It's Getting Hot in Here:**
   Towards an Erotics of Climate Change

› **Choose Your Own Banality**
   A new book series for tweens

› **The Most Notorious PowerPoint Presentations in History**

› **Bleeding-Harp Liberal:**
   The Implicit Politics of Joanna Newsom's Lyrics

If you masturbate on a plane, does that make you a member of the Half-Mile High Club?

The world has officially jumped the shark, on this day, July 18, 2006. Today's headline: "Brad Pitt happy to hear Shiloh's burp."

Devastation can lie dormant in a sugar bowl, when seen in the right light.

More important than a good life coach is a good death coach. After all, we seem very ill equipped to deal with our own finitude.

Something about hyper-capital requires its minions to be frayed and afraid. For some reason this lubricates the machine better. The less functional you feel, the more functional you actually are.

The years go fast, but the weeks go slow.

There is a huge difference between "just 'cause" and "just cause."

"I would never do that." Says person, just about to do that.

Perhaps it's better to fail effortlessly, than succeed with great effort.

Is it a truism that the more sophisticated life becomes, the more petty and pathetic? Or are humans an aberration?

Alien anthropologists and archaeologists of the future will wonder why the relatively benign Bush Snr years produced music with the sonic and lyrical intensity of Nirvana, Helmet, Rage Against the Machine, Tool, Pantera, PJ Harvey, Public Enemy, Bodycount, etc. Whereas the current austerity regime has produced Bon Iver, Sufjan Stevens, Mumford and Sons, Bright Eyes, and all those ukelele lala clappety clap, Brooklyn bands.

Every week I stand in front of semi-strangers, and make conceptual balloon animals in the air. For this I get paid.

It seems that some people's dreams have a "budget" equivalent to late Kurosawa or James Cameron; featuring thousands of extras, and sweeping, panoramic dreamwork cinematography. Whereas my dreams almost always have a budget closer to late Vince Gallo, or some unknown mumblecore director.

There's only a 45-degree-angle difference between a bad committee meeting and *The Human Centipede*.

CHILD: "Daddy, why does the rainbow make colors?"
FATHER: "Google it."

This coffee shop is playing a Morrissey album. No wonder the milk in my coffee has soured.

It used to be the case that "90% of life is just showing up." Now 90% of life is answering emails.

Can't we just montage the rest of the semester?

The Seducer's allure:
"Don't you see? I can make you *especially* miserable."

Someone could make a fortune offering lap dance haircuts.

Spare a thought for the Victorian paparazzi:
"Miss Lind. Miss Lind. Please stand still for ten minutes!"

Downton Abby erotic fan fiction, chapter 17: "Lady Mary Seduces Carson After Too Much Sherry."

Humans *are* the time being.

Of course yesterday was better than today. There have been hundreds of thousands of yesterdays, and only one today.

New York wouldn't be New York without insomnia.

Gay men think outside the box.

And the Nookie Monster sings: Q is for Quickie, that's good enough for me.

Today I seem to be suffering from an acute case of whatsthepointitis.

Why do we strive to make plans fool-proof? Shouldn't they be genius-proof?

I'm extremely sylph-conscious.

Before pulling the trigger, the high-priced hitman insisted on payment via a Swiss bank account, a forged US passport, and a spousal hire.

Imagine how different the world would be if we thought of ourselves as mediums, rather than vessels. Lifted would be the burden of retaining information, for a start.

Irony #345,671: Just at the historical moment when nothing is actually happening anymore, everyone is scrambling to make documentary movies. There is a collective urge to capture the non-events of today.

Yet more evidence of the moralism which permeates scientific discourse. Bacteria on the human body has now been classed as "residents" vs. "transients," with the latter being more harmful.

It's amazing what can happen when a dirty mind meets a clean body.

Australia = the real
Europe = the imaginary
Asia = the symbolic
    +
North America = the hyperreal
South America = the surreal
Africa = the infrareal

Grading is degrading.

Musicians play a work, while playwrights work on a play.

It's time to invent a new musical genre: humble hip hop.

Earth: A nice place to visit, but I wouldn't want to live there.

When I grow up, I want to be a transcendental hygienist.

A motorcycle is just two unicycles tied together, then strapped to an engine.

You don't have to believe in yourself. You just have to look like you do.

Academics are the most insane people on Earth. They voluntarily, of their own free will, give themselves assignments, essays and homework all year round, for the rest of their lives.

Last night a DJ mildly improved my life.

Calling someone "egocentric" is like calling them "carbon-based."

Q: What do you call a hip person who studies too much?
A: A fly swat.

That thing where you compose the world's most glowing letter of recommendation, in your mind, while walking home from the subway… for yourself.

Blaming a person for a fit of anger or passion is a bit like asking a valley why a tornado raged through it.

Q: What do you call a man proud of his balls?
A: Egotesticle.

Do you think if baboons were into social networking, they would have Assbook instead of Facebook?

Did our grandparents suffer from propeller-lag?

What hell to be an emoticon. Trapped in the one affective state constantly.

In the American remake of *Black Mirror*, Steve Carell plays the President who, instead of enduring the humiliation of having sex with a pig on live TV, is instead obliged to give an intern health insurance.

There's much more to being sexy than "being sexy."

"And on the seventh day, God became really morose, and couldn't be bothered to do much, and felt the world he'd just created wasn't any good anyway."

Scared of flying? Really?! I mean, what's the worst than can happen?

My life is full of plot holes.

Musetrap.

Everything has a capability. And at some point everything loses that capability.

The genius of religion is linking the sense of the sublime with a moral code, where in fact no such connection need exist.

What's yellow and really wants a book deal?
A.W. Pee.

Australia is the Galapagos Islands of snack foods.

It's never too early to start getting ahead of yourself.

Television has a bad case of the re-runs.

The dogma ate my Gesamtkunstwerk.

"Come to the New York Public Library and read between the lions."

We all live in the present, tense.

We reward the one we love by giving them less physical, psychological, emotional, and spiritual latitude than we give anyone else in the world. How fucked up is that!

How sad that one's feelings later in life aren't sweeter and more mellow, like a late harvest Riesling. Instead, they almost inevitably turn to vinegar.

Slow and steady wins the race...unless it's the 100 meters.

Did medieval monasteries have an "exorcise yard"?

A shame that God didn't also provide Moses with "The Ten Suggestions" (e.g., 1. Always dry between your toes after a shower or bath, etc.).

Some of the best female impersonators out there are women.

One of the core character traits of women — suspicion — is such because they are obliged, from a very early age, to play vigilant chaperone to their own bodies. They have thus little choice but to be the spinster aunt to themselves.

Is it possible to declare one's love without including a stamped, self-addressed envelope?

Yes, nature and culture is a false distinction. But would you rather wake up to the sound of chirping, conversing birds or beeping, reversing trucks?

Turns out the committee that gave Obama the Nobel Peace Prize also gave Agamemnon a World's Best Dad coffee mug.

I only just realized that a "vicarious experience" is not necessarily the kind of experience that a vicar might have.

I am below reproach.

Do strippers, porn stars, or "life models" have nightmares about showing up to work fully clothed?

I put the "rock" in bureaucracy.

Does Jesus sometimes wonder what he himself would do?

Do you think The Beatles song "Let It Be" was actually sponsored by the CIA to promote *laissez-faire* capitalism?

Judging by the conversations I hear on the streets of New York, two thirds of the young women of this city consistently fail the Bechdel Test.

What a blessing it is (or rather, would be) to not be obliged to have something to say.

In terms of one's psyche, a sense of possibility is far more important than actual achievements.

You can say what you like about me, but I can pour two glasses of wine at exactly the same level, first go, almost every time.

Healing two birds with one bird-healing kit.

Flagellation is just a long word for pride.

Who do the Joneses try to keep up with?

How many fully-fledged assholes are mistaken for "kind of an asshole"?

When it comes to moderation, I am an extremist.

It must be admitted that I'm flappable.

Freud was right about penis envy. Just not about the gender who suffers from it.

In order to grow, one must deal with shit. You can't spell *Bildungsroman* without "dung."

It's amusing when men proudly boast, "I've never paid for sex." Yes they have. Just not with money.

Etsy clothes designers are often muslin extremists.

The paradox or principle of Buridan's Ass means that Abercrombie and/or Fitch would escape meeting me without a black eye. I simply wouldn't know who to punch first.

I aspire to be a lad who lunches.

Expect little from life and it will happily oblige.

I have high friends in places.

We are all acorns. There is no tree.*

---

* I think I was high when I wrote this one, because I now have no idea what I meant by it. Perhaps some kind reader can explain it to me?

The would-be post-capitalist condition: An incredulity toward brand narratives.

All my sins are terribly unoriginal.

Time to write my Statement of Purposelessness.

I can't believe it's not democracy!

Shouldn't Hermes sell messenger bags?

I don't have a receding hairline. Other men just have preceding hairlines.

Q: What's brown and sticky?
A: Poo.

Q: What's worse than a giraffe with a sore neck?
A: Genocide.

Flattery is the insincerest form of imitation.

Rosario: Patron Saint of waitresses who weep silently while taking your order on Christmas.

On Achilles: "But who dies from an arrow wound to the ankle?"

First rule of Music Club: If this song could feasibly be featured on a Sofia Coppola soundtrack, then avoid at all costs.

What if species itself is an example of the narcissism of minor differences?

With *Maldoror*, Lautréamont humps the shark.

The other day I insulted a vampire. He was immortally offended.

SUI GENEROUS (Latin phrase) — an act of kindness, seemingly out of nowhere.

It is one thing to use one's thoughts to reinforce a feeling, opinion, or prejudice. Quite another to actually think.

One's spouse is like an old remote control. She or he becomes less and less responsive, so that one has to push harder and harder. Nevertheless, one cannot imagine life without them.

In space, no-one can hear you scream. On earth, everyone can. But nobody is going to do anything about it.

Australia has a Plague Locust Commission. Even the apocalypse is now bureaucratic.

To fall out of love is to render the former beloved back to a simple piece of the global jigsaw puzzle; rather than representing the image to which all the other pieces previously combined to reveal.

We used to suffer from the blues. Now we suffer from the blahs.

Italy's new tourism slogan is "Spend Your Money In Italy." Really.

Theology asks why Adam was tempted into eating the apple. Physics asks why the apple hit Newton on the head. Metaphysics asks if Steve Jobs had a soul.

To seduce without the aid of magic potions. #nophiltre

Buff historian.

I suffer from attitude sickness.

Evil word of the day: "sublethal." As in BP's safety policy report that describes any oil spill as probably "sublethal" to marine life.

The dry cleaner ruined my birthday suit!

The former founder of the foundation's fund was fond of fondling foundlings.

There is madness to my method.

I have enough sour grapes to make an entire cellar of disgusting wine.

Rilke's lesser known *Letters to a Millennial*.

The genius of Kurt Cobain: anti-macho testosterone.

The virtual = the test(es) of time.

They must have a lot of union issues in Hollywood, with all those scripts that write themselves.

Freud would be a lot more relevant to the average person today if he had called it the MILF complex.

It's like there's a party in my mouth, and none of you are invited.

George Steiner writes: "The orgasm is an exclamation mark." However, I'd say it's more of an asterisk.

I hope at least one of my breakdowns is sanguine, rather than nervous.

Sometimes I think Americans invented baseball purely as a rich source of metaphors for daily life.

I'm pretty sure she wasn't into me, since she was redressing me with her eyes.

The phrase "I have too many tabs open" meant something very different in the 70s.

The USA is a global superpower with a provincial soul.

uPhone™ — making the world as remote and opaque as you always suspected it was!

There are two ways to lie in bed, and they are often found together.

People often refer to me as the eight hundred thousand two hundred and fifty-third Beatle.

Unlike Bono, I *did* find what I was looking for... however I soon lost it again behind the fridge.

I religiously observe secular holidays.

Tempted to finally buy myself a Nintendo console for Christmas, so I can play Wii Committee Meeting during the holiday break.

Finding your true lust is even rarer than finding your true love.

Budget as body: death by a thousand cuts.

Squirrels: Nature's parkour.

Why do they still call it "gentrification"? It's not as if neighborhoods are being taken over by the gentry. Instead they should call it "douchification" or "wankification."

My dream last night had a DVD menu pointing to Bonus Features.

Kicking names and taking ass.

Epitaphs are just blurbs for dead people.

Connoisseur of unilateral frisson.

My dreams are pretty much all B-roll.

The world is full of sentimental reptiles.

Sad fact: If you think to yourself "I've still got it"—you probably don't.

I just finished watching *The Martian*. If I wanted to watch an unpleasant man eat a potato every day, then I'd prefer to watch Bela Tarr's *Turin Horse*.

The unfolding of neo-liberalism: at age 13, I was masturbating to images of Madonna. At age 39 I found myself working for her.

How much should you tip someone who saves your life?

Sexual identity is an oxymoron. We have sex to shatter our identities. It's an all-too-brief release from being who we are. Which is why we crave it so.

It takes a village (to deal with village idiots).

JFK came-a-lot.

Bread and Circuses → Red Bull and Reality TV.

Don't assume that emoticon is happy, just because it's smiling. Look into its eyes! Can't you see the desperation therein?

Academics could learn a lot from the gangsters in film noir: whatever you do, try to avoid getting "the chair."

Freud reverses Funkadelic: "Free your ass, and your mind will follow."

Is "working out" at the gym some kind of Freudian compromise between acting out and working through?

There but for the spite of God go I.

Q: What did the necrophiliac say when asked about his love life?
A: I'm seeing dead people.

Jean-Paul Sartre's narrator felt a profound, existential nausea when looking upon a tree trunk. I feel the same way when looking upon a Hollister t-shirt.

Whoever said money can't buy you happiness obviously never bought a cocktail.

The three most beautiful words in the English language—"Ok—you win."

Who are the worst, most annoying gentrifiers on the planet? Humans!

Forget Italian stallions! The discerning lover wants an Australian mammalian.

I guess I'm just not selfish enough to have kids.

Humanity is fast becoming little more than a biological substrate for advertising.

They say that men are only after one thing; but it's simply not true. They're after three or four things.

Apparently the universe is still "an adolescent," if we consider where it is along the timescale of its lifespan. No wonder it's so annoying!

Snark is the blue-green algae of discourse.

I was working out at the gym and a big guy covered in muscles came up to me and grunted, "Hey, can you spot me?" To which I replied, "Sure. You're right there!"

Grown men — weeping on ellipticals.

The laws of Sisyphysics.

Humans could not live without tree flatulence.

Life's biggest irony is that "life" gets in the way of living. In other words, "making a living" is anything but.

Who said methodology can't be sexy? — "Show me what you're working with!"

Dear funding body, attached is my six word proposal: "Just give me some f%#&ing money!"

My nature abhors vacuuming.

Henceforth, all white-cube art galleries in gentrified areas are to be known as "douche portals."

Angels exist. But they are simply people, who come to your aid when you most need it.

"Love laughs at locksmiths," goes the old saying. But it weeps at security experts.

What year was love privatized?

I'm suffering from a very rare condition called "life." And an even rarer complication of this called "consciousness."

What is a gravy train anyway? And does its schedule correspond to the gravy boat?

If a risk is worth taking, then it's not really a risk.

"Budgie smugglers," "bingo wings," "map o'Tassie"—
the vulgar genius of Australian slang.

The bearable heaviness of doing.

Is there anything more annoying than opinions?
Including this one?

I gave my entourage the day off today.

In the (near) future, everyone will give a 15-minute TED Talk.

How do you know when you're listening to *bad* jazz?

LET'S PLAY
BAM NEXT WAVE FESTIVAL BINGO!

- ☑ **The Gondwanaland Dance Ensemble**

- ☑ **The Legibly Ethnic Jazz Choir**

- ☑ **The Stubbornly Untranslated Steam-Puppets of Myanmar**

- ☑ **Laurie Anderson makes sonic shadow-poems with David Byrne's laurels**

- ☑ **Steve Reich debuts new aural triptych about fracking the soul with three quarters of the Kronos Quartet**

- ☑ **Tilda Swinton appears in a one person show critiquing the inevitable gendering of the color beige**

- ☑ **Ira Glass vs. Philip Glass in an allegorical capoeira grudge match**

- ☑ **Radiolab broadcast live from Wes Anderson's butterfly atrium**

- ☑ **Spike Lee grumpily tells a room full of happily ashamed white people to go back to Manhattan**

BINGO!

How do you know if you're talking to a *rude* German?

I wonder if the dish regrets not running off with the fork.

It's always 1986 in small-town Europe.

Naughty by nurture.

Greta Garbo answered Freud's infamous question: "What does woman want?"

Terrorforming: the act by which governments use fear to reconfigure the environment for maximum control of the populace.

To a hammer, everything looks like a nail. To a middle-aged tourist, everything looks like a toilet.

Parisians on their way home from work, brandishing baguettes like swords against the perils of domestic ennui.

Once we run out of oil, we won't have a car in the world.

It's really hard. Like shooting barrels with fish.

Dionysus never Apollogizes.

I left my smart phone in my smart car while I was buying some smart water. How stupid of me!

When I was a kid I thought the future would be jet packs and holograms. But it turned out to involve waving one's arms frenetically in the cafe toilet, so the motion-detecting lights will turn back on.

Ivan the Not-So-Bad.

Marzipan is the Australian guest of flavors (i.e., tolerated, but not exactly welcome).

If hell is other people, then Facebook is Satan's Rolodex.

It's up to you whether you see the glass as nine-tenths empty or one-tenth full.

It was one of the worst cases of inflation since the middle ages, when a horse cost precisely one kingdom.

This pick-me-up let me down.

I'm skeptical that mammoths had that many tasks to do.

I'd like to get another beer, but it's a fridge too far.

What if psychoanalysis did not begin with "a child is being beaten," but rather "a child is beat-boxing"?

Why does nothing take so long to happen?

You can't make an *hommelette* without dividing some zygotes.

"Evolution will eventually be televised." —Darwin

Paradise would have Italian coffee, French bread, and Japanese toilets.

Sometimes — while doing nothing in particular — I have an inexplicable urge to be in Mumbai's hottest nightclub.

78% of self-described "cool" aunties and uncles not actually cool, finds new report.

Love is the feeling you create in order to smother the sense of hostility you now have for someone, after realizing how much you need them.

Action speaks louder than words. But inaction speaks louder than action.

At court, Kurt would curtly and covertly curtsy as a courtesy.

Political economy as French detective novel: *cherchez l'ouvrier*.

[Overheard in New York] "The sex with him just felt soooo *right*...I guess that's why it was so boring."

Your true self is a performance so convincing that even *you* buy it.

Forget the Higgs Boson stuff. CERN made another big discovery last week, as they determined the exact nano-point that something becomes "so bad it's good."

Why is there something and not nothing? And why is that something so God damn stupid?

Why always try so hard to keep "on top of things"? It's like being locked in the missionary position with life.

It's square to be hip.

The realistic ethnic stereotype hooker: "Me love you average amount of time."

Hertz-on-Demand: a rival to Zip Car? Or a new S&M cable channel?

The world is my oyster. But I'm allergic to shellfish.

'Pataphysics: The science of imaginary solutions.
Psychoanalysis: The science of imaginary problems.

Today's nuanced and devastating critique of capitalism was brought to you by Verizon.

I am an anti-social butterfly.

I wonder if humans will evolve "like" buttons in their navels, so when someone says something popular, others can press them, and they light up.

I'm genuinely curious to know what millennials will find annoying about the generation that follows them.

It ain't easy to maintain this churlish figure.

Except for a handful of best-selling authors, shouldn't it be called a "peasantry check"?

All these people doing the Lord's work. Makes me think God was the original outsourcer.

I volunteer to be chair of the poetic justice committee.

Loser-generated content.

"Crowd sourcing" is so 2011. Now I'm in to "sauced crowding."

Jean Michel Jarre's "Oxygène" is the thinking person's "Popcorn."

The teenager is a human creature who is precisely 50% annoying and 50% annoyed.

In medieval Wales, pretty much everything was "easier done than said."

I put a whole jar of glitter into my bath this evening, to lift my spirits and make me feel better. But it all just sank to the bottom, clumped around my nether-hairs, and gave me a rash.

Most tweets are really squawks.

Somewhere around your late 30s, the stupigens in your system begin to turn into crankigens.

Exhausted from donating my body to social science.

Don't blame the gypsies. Unless you're absolutely sure.

Classical philologists sheepishly admit that the original translation is "Achilles' Penis."

I'm concerned about the world's scruple-to-qualm ratio.

Forget fossil fuels. This economy runs mostly on delusion.

Cetaceans are the most amazing creatures. They are a whole class of animal that just said: "Fuck it. We're going back to the ocean. I don't care if we can't breathe under water. We'll just gulp air near the top. Whatever it takes to avoid that whole land-hand nonsense anymore. That's for suckers."

I have Tinder feelings towards you.

I had a dream last night that I broke up a fight between two sunflowers.

My wife recently said to me: "You're so clever!...You should be more clever."

The vast distance between being alive and feeling alive.

Humans are the animal that thinks that it can think differently to how it thinks.

I do love the human element. I'm just not convinced it's actually human.

Behold, the ghost of conversations stopped suddenly halfway through, because another friend arrived at the scene, never to be completed.

Interlocutorbook: Social Networking for the Insufferably Pretentious.

Later today I intend to surprise myself with an intravention.

When will the animal kingdom become an animal republic?

In Walter Benjamin's day, "hash-tagging" simply meant labeling one's stash.

Q: What did Hydrogen say to Water?
A: I am your father. That is your *density!*

Newspaper headline: "Billionaires Admit That They Have Been Keeping African-Americans Poor Just For All The Great Music."

For a thorough existential workout, be sure to work on your isolation.

Enthusiasm is always over-enthusiasm.

Isn't it interesting that we are quick to denounce slavery — the ownership of one person by another — yet just as quick to celebrate marriage.

Solitaire? Two can play at *that* game!

Sadly, I will never drunkenly, bitterly punch my own passé hit single into a juke-box in a San Francisco dive bar. #elusive-bucket-list-items-inspired-by-the-valley-of-the-dolls

Porn: a global methadone program for sex addicts.

If you ever happen to be tempted to entertain a glimmer of hope for the future of the human race, then check out the perma-line to get into Abercrombie & Fitch on Fifth Avenue.

Why has Foucault's pendulum been swinging for centuries without stopping, but this hammock I'm currently lazing in comes to a standstill within two or three minutes?

Deleuze helped vintage philosophy breathe. He was a de-Kanter.

Older people are spoiler alerts for the next generation.

Is America so anti-erotic because everyone works so hard? Or does everyone work so hard because America is so anti-erotic?

Occam's Aftershave: For when you don't want to get lathered up by unlikely possibilities.

If Sergio Leone made "Spaghetti Westerns," does that mean Dario Argento made "Fettuccini Horrors?"

Quicksand was a much bigger problem in the 1970s than it is today. At least on TV.

As soon as we hear talk of "preserving" something or other, whether it be a building or a species or a way of life, we can be sure it's already lost.

Facebook; or as they call it in France: « Le grand livre qui rassemble un mélange de visages mondiaux. »

Gothenburg Syndrome: When you originally like your kidnappers, but then — after prolonged captivity — decide they are idiots, and want nothing to do with their worldview.

Why be a vulgar Marxist when you can be an obscene one?

Less is more.
Unless it's cake.

Life is a biological typo.

Elephants are too polite to mention the human in the room.

Why can't people be like leaves, dying in luminous, resplendent color and beauty?

Humanity: you're doing it wrong.

White-cube art galleries are the urban equivalent of Dutch elm disease.

Continental philosophers use the word "precisely" precisely to the extent that what they are saying is not precise.

In nineteenth-century France, married women who refused to take a lover or become a mistress were shamed into wearing a scarlet letter M on their clothing, in order to tell all the world that they were that pitiful creature, a "monogamist."

For every writer there are 0.031 readers.

Can anything other than heights wuther?

My gym membership is one of the few frozen things unthreatened by climate change.

I have invented a new methodology for literary criticism, which involves *literally* reading between the lines.

Thus far, I have discovered that Shakespeare was really telling us this: "   "
And Woolf was telling us this: "   "
Whereas Pynchon is now telling us this: "   ."

Companies love misery.

Accident is the niece of invention.

Don't make me get early modern on yo ass!

Is it true that clouds are lonely?

Rock me, Salieri.

Welcome to our beautiful city's Histrionic District.

Who you are is to a very large extent *where* you are.
(cf. Kurosawa's *Dursu Urzula*)

Mother Earth is bipolar.

Modernity: when we started turning crosses into telephone poles.

There is no sexual relation. Exhibit #238:
"Why wouldn't she?" vs. "why would I?"

Lust is *because*, love *despite*.

Listening to M83's "Skin of the Night" is like drowning in the delicious lime-pink honey of neon bees.

I am suspicious of most common sense. But impressed with much folk wisdom.

Slogan for a crematorium: "Life: Urn it."

Good for the soul, bad for the skin.

The biggest curse in life is thinking that it owes you something.

Kafka Hotel: there is soap, but not for us.

Boys are more heartless than girls. Women are more heartless than men.

A sentence is worth 1.2% of a photograph.

The missionary position is a WASP fetish. It's just so common that it doesn't seem like one.

Someone needs to stem this tidal wave of American immigration into New York City.

I have a very steep forgetting curve.

Feeling combobulated.

All the world is a stage (the universe is going through).

Bookish girls with dewey decimal faces.

Kate Bush's first hit single was based on a classic of nineteenth-century literature. If only Carly Rae Jepsen's first song was "Call Me Ishmael."

That neither pleasant nor unpleasant low-level body hum that accompanies a job well done — a job that has absolutely nothing to do with your *raison d'être*.

When I'm really old, I'm going to sing in an alt.barbershop-quartet called The Gentlemen Callers.

Metaphysics — the move from the meaning of life to the meaning of the meaning of life.

"Turn me on."
This phrase suggests that the default setting for humans is "off."

The profound peace and contentment one feels when surrounded by enough toilet paper to last several weeks.

Stage-name: Paige Turner.

They know not what they do not do.

Love = emotional insurance scam.

Bar Life — the state of exceptional intoxication.

And in a dark twist worthy of *Black Mirror*, ISIS turn out to be a crack viral marketing team working for HBO to promote their new show about terrorism.

My issue with empiricism: Is there anything less interesting than a verfiable truth?

Surely the real takeaway from *Breaking Bad* is that *anything* is better than being a teacher.

(//_-)
Putting the "emo" in emoticon.

Old Chinese Curse:
"May you get what you want. But in the wrong color!"

Oxymoron of the day: a singular groupie.

A mating of the minds.

The best things in life are those that we can't possibly justify.
(cf. writing)

The pensive pleasure of staring out the window at the snow, ruined by dude in the opposite building, doing the same.

A good measure of how inebriated you are is whether you start thinking or saying, "New York *is* pretty great, isn't it?!"

The Alchemist, The Secret, The Life of Pi, The Unbearable Lightness of Being, The Girl With the Dragon Tattoo, The Da Vinci Code, and a bunch of other middle-brow staples.
(a.k.a., The Library of Alexandra)

"Hello, sir. A pleasure to meet you. I'm the fly that will be in your ointment today."

Old Russian birdwatcher in Central Park: "Yes. I watch the birds. They do not give me happiness.... But for a moment, they can give me less sadness."

Cruel optimization.

The *real* Turing Test will be when androids laugh at fart noises.

When I hear a colleague described as a "flight risk" I think of sunglasses, forged passports, code-phrases, secret drop-off points, and lipstick left on barely-sipped coffee in steam-filled train-stations.

Weep not for those things you cut, but became distracted before pasting. And thus confine to oblivion.

Literature: show don't tell.
Politics: tell don't show.

Small-batch, artisanal Theory.

When did "becoming a thing" become a thing?

Are you more likely to be found:
1) opening some wine
2) whining at some opening

Humans are so adorable. They think they're people!

Music is thawed architecture.

"Waiting for Goffman: Face Work in the Age of Botox."

Writing is really easy. Rewriting, really hard.

I'm not sure what's more annoying: not being asked to participate in things, or being asked to participate in things.

Human delusion #356: Wearing too little on a chilly day in early Spring, as this itself will convince the weather to be much warmer than forecast.

Summer city parks must be a hazard for the jazz-intolerant.

Scientists have recently confirmed that moderate, regular doses of alcohol creates a significant increase of abilitytocopeagens in the bloodstream.

Economy = saving up.
Ecology = saving for.

Australia is the world's Florida.

When you turn your pillow over in the the middle of the night, it's like flipping over to Side Two of your dreams.

If you are using social media to talk about that special woman in your life, be sure to tweet her right.

Was Bogart the only film star who became a verb?

Does anyone know how to take a screen-cap of my dreams?

Did you hear about the woman who couldn't divide numbers in half?
She literally couldn't even.

When it comes to climate change, I'm extremely pessimistic. I am sure that humans will be on this Earth for a long time yet.

It staggers me how the US government can simply ignore infrastructure, and hope the place keeps going without collapsing completely. It's as if America believes that all these cities were truly built on nothing but rock 'n' roll.

It's amazing how easy it is to not do things.

So, I built it. And no-one came.

I am a permanent resident of indignation.

Two birds in Central Park, both with binoculars and consulting a book called "What Human Is That?"

BIRD 1: "I think that's a Pot-bellied Northern-European Wanker."
BIRD 2: "No. I'm pretty sure it's a Quiffed Mid-Western Douche."

A "d" is a reverse "p." Which is why a dimple is the opposite of a pimple.

They say a pleasure shared is a pleasure doubled. Unless it's sex. Then it's, like, quadrupled.

The very presence of a whiteboard means your endeavor is doomed.

Perhaps our compressed corpses will be fuel for the vehicles of some other creature in a billion years or so.

A book of psalms for athiests.

The New York dating scene is for the feint of heart.

Q: What do they call the stupidest viking on the expedition?
A: The pillage idiot.

Melodrama be like:
"We can't."
"But we must."
"But we can't."
"But we must."
"Yes we must."
"But we can't."
"No we can't."
"But we did. That one time."
"Almost."
"Yes, almost."
"But we musn't again."
"Even though we didn't quite."
"Yes."
"No."
"Certainly."

Taking a tip from Tolstoy, I always speak French at dinner, so the servants cannot follow the conversation.

I think I need a retreat from writing.

The world means the world to me.

"Inaffective Labor: Duane Reade and the Strategic (Dis)simulation of Service"

The croissant I will eat for breakfast tomorrow doesn't exist yet. This makes me happy, for some reason.

Q: How did the fashion designer spend his time at the nudist colony?
A: Dressing everyone with his eyes.

Different cities have a different flavor of potentiality in the refreshing hour or so after dawn. In Paris, the morning time brings the promise of an impromptu romance. In Tokyo, a business deal sealed. In Rome, the promise of intrigue and decadence. In Berlin, the promise of an intellectual epiphany. In Madrid, an aesthetic one. In Istanbul, a spiritual one. And in New York, it is the frisson created by the sense that someone's life is surely going to get royally screwed today, along with the breathless hope that it isn't yours.

I've said it before. So I won't say it again.

The lesson of Timothy Treadwell: we all have a bear to cross.

Perhaps Israel would feel less anxious if their neighbors felt they belonged to Palestein.

Beastie Boys lyrics that never were:
"I feel dem high-art movies,
like my man Stan Brakhage,
all my shorties grab their phone
to report my suspicious package"

Alas, poor your dick,
I knew him, fellatio.

Q: What did the bank manager say to Ann and Nancy Wilson?
A: How can I get you a loan?

Person wearing a button that says: "Ask me about why I don't want to talk to you."

"I hope you're civic-minded, because you've just been summoned for booty duty."

We return you now to our regularly scheduled pogrom.

I'm starting to wonder if ABBA were in fact a sly homage to their celebrated compatriot, Ingmar Bergman.

All curators are exhibitionists.

Sitting under a tree in Central Park yesterday, I saw a fledgling robin trying to fly for the first time. This avian-in-training was clinging on to a twig-like branch for dear life, as the wind buffeted it to and fro. It would vacillate between standing grimly still, like a stuffed bird, and then stretching its wings in anxious preparation for the big leap. Its mother, losing patience with waiting, would call to it from the nearby tree, to which the baby bird would tweet back in exasperation and fear. A couple of times it defecated, and even regurgitated, surely due to nerves. Eventually, the mother flew over and essentially pushed her offspring off the branch, so the latter managed to flap its way over to another tree, at which time the process started all over again.

So much for "hard-wired" behavior, and the machinic grace of instinctive nature. We're all just trying to figure things out, and a lot of it is terrifying — even (maybe especially) to a tiny birdbrain. Of course our genes prepare us for many events and behaviors. But the actuality of the present moment, and all its contingent affordances, mean that our "character" is put to the test; and while some flourish, others fail (and others inhabit the wide spectrum in between).

The Gauloise cigarette packets in France now feature a warning which translates as: "Smoking harms your own health, and the health of your entourage."

I belong to the SFAA—the Society for the Abolition of Acronyms.

Q: What's round, brown, and fertilizes the Garden of Eden?
A: Eve's droppings.

Q: What's the best way to film a donut?
A: With a cinnamontographer.

Buffet, the Diet Slayer.

Q: What do you call someone who claims that they have repaired your car, but you're not really sure if this is true?
A: A quantum mechanic.

Watch like no-one's dancing.

Duran Duran's non-awaited comeback.

If love is blind, then sex is Braille.

73% of conversations between co-habitants go something like this:
"We need another X."
"Do we though?"
"Yes."
"I suppose you're right."
"Can we afford it?"
"Not really. But we really need it."
"I know. Can't you find it cheap on Craig's List or something?"
"You get what you pay for."
"True. But we don't need top-of-the-line do we?"
"Not necessarily. But it's often a false economy to just buy a cheap one you need again soon."
Sigh.
"I guess. Screw it then. We'll get a decent X."
"Dammit!"
"What now?!"
"I just broke the Y. We're going to need a new Y."

Bored of Education.

Q: What did the typographer say when her boyfriend was being marginalized?
A: Justify my love.

I put down the phone. ("You stupid phone! You're a no good phone!") Then I poured myself a whisky.

Happy Angst-Giving.

It's a little known fact that the *Egyptian Book of the Dead* was actually the sequel to the best-selling *Egyptian Book of the Seriously Unwell*.

It would be funny to call your first album, "The Best Of…"

And as Nietzsche says, many happy returns.

The Nobel Prize for Pornography.

It's better to nurse an injury than injure a nurse.

There's no taste for accounting.

"The Man of Soul Under Socialism: The Influence of Motown on Soviet Pop Music."

Sure, every cloud has a silver lining. But every ointment comes with a fly.

Walking around the corridors of an Ivy League English department feels like you need a zoological guide by your side: "And here we have one of the world's finest specimens of an early modernist. Next to her we have this fine fellow, a stunning example of a medievalist. Now if you turn your attention over here you can see a very impressive nineteeth-century Americanist…no…wait…oh, he's sleeping…"

Old habitats are easy to break.

Bemused louche.

A strangler is just a fiend you haven't met yet.

New writing tip or trick. Start each section or chapter with analytical or theoretical equivalents of those proleptic summaries from Victorian novels: "Chapter 5: In which Uncle Roger realizes the folly of his stubborn ways, abandons the coconut raft which made young Sally so fatigued, and decamps to the other side of the island, just as the signal fire is discovered by pirates."

It's impossible to feel "at home" in New York City, because it is the world's anti-home. That's why people come here. To feel productively un-homed.

THE NAUGHTY CLOSET
NEWSLETTER FOR APRIL

New XXX Titles

› **Lawrence of a Labia**

› **The Divine Connerie**

› **Saving Ryan's Privates**

› **Travels with My Arse**

› **The Loin King**

› **All That Jizz**

› **Look Who Came On Dinner**

› **In Golden Pond**

› **Raiders of the Lost Arse**

› **Dr. Quim Medicine Woman** (*seniors*)

› **Wanking Life**

› **Seven Brides for One Brother** (*Mormon fetish*)

› **Dawson's Crack**

› **Fiddler on the Roof**

(cont'd, over)

Marquee Names from the new burlesque show

"Uncle Vanya and the Three Sisters in the Cherry Orchard"

(*playing in the store's backroom on Saturday evenings in November*)

- › **Tawdry Hepburn**
- › **Mother Goosed**
- › **Snatch Victory**
- › **Oedipal Panties**
- › **Alison Wonderland**
- › **Polly Amory**

New Books of Interest

- › **Neurotica**: Sexy Stories for Self-Conscious and High-Strung People
- › **From Nymph Loads to Lymph Nodes:** A Mythico-Physiological History of Arousal
- › **A Sphincter is Haunting Europe** (a.k.a., The Origin of Feces)
- › **Drinking Bottomless Coffee in Assless Chaps**
- › **The Male Glaze**: A Cultural History of Semen

Another day, another neo-liberal "solution" to problems caused by neo-liberalism.

Is there anything more humble and wonderful than a wooden spoon?

Due to an unfortunate typo, I spent my teen years at an English hoarding school.

They say that revenge is best served cold. But most vengeful chefs now agree that the ideal temperature should be lukewarm: around 40 degrees Fahrenheit.

Surely a divorce registry makes more sense. It's the unhappy couple that need nice presents.

Georges Bataille, that paragon of political correctness, claimed that old women are depressing to behold because there is no exciting visual contrast between the freshness of the face and wrinkled aspect of the genitals. For the same reason, bald men should not wear turtlenecks.

Today's epiphany: tennis is just Pong with people.

France, to its credit, was the only country that assimilated mimes, rather than exterminating them.

To be anti-theory because of jargon is like being anti-music because of Nickelback.

The transitional weeks between Summer and Fall are most accurately measured by the gin-to-bourbon ratio.

It was very recently that humanity took a completely wrong turn. With Socrates, that is.

A bottle of wine is a Marshall stack in disguise: amplifying the acoustic emotions buried in the blood a hundredfold.

A man suffers from Surprise-Party Syndrome, so that every room he enters, he's convinced his friends and family are waiting inside, ready to jump from behind the furniture and yell "SURPRISE!!"...he even looks behind the sofa, and seems genuinely bewildered when he doesn't find anyone.

Flattery is like fossil fuel. We feel it is essential to get through the day, but we also know that it will run out at some point.

Erotic website idea for academics: an attractive bookish woman or a charming bespectacled man talking directly to a webcam, and saying: "Yes. Yes. You've got tenure!"

Marriage: two different people suffering from the same multiple-personality disorder.

Love wreck-tangle.

She was like plutonium that didn't want to be weaponized. A sex-bomb that wanted to defuse itself before exploding.

Expecting the libido to perform in wedlock is like expecting a circus to perform in a courtroom.

Infidelity? Polyfidelity!

Tales of a vanilla pervert.

Could it be that tattoos are for people that never want to be naked?

High fructose porn syrup.

The happy couple: he, in a sports bar; she in a sports bra.

He was a handsome cad in a hansom cab.

"I feel like a man trapped in a man's body."
(*Mom*, season 1, episode 7)

The economy has got so bad. Last week I was mugged by my doorman.

Inbox Sisyphus.

The bidet is a rather proud and prosaic object. It seems to say to any foreigner in its vicinity: "Yes, we have a lot of sex in Europe. What of it?"

The terrible thing about beauty is that it does not belong to the one in which it is (currently) embodied.

John Cage's famous quote "I have nothing to say—and I'm saying it" doesn't seem nearly so profound in the age of Facebook and Twitter.

She plays chard rock in a vegan metal band.

Everything happens for a reason. Usually a bad reason.

All caps thoughts kept me up all night.

Overheard chauvinist: "All that bluestocking, suffragette, Virginia Woolf nonsense! Give them a *broom* of their own, I say, and they should be grateful!"

2-star Michelin lunch becomes 1-star Michelin feces.

I have a monogrammed handkerchief and a handy monograph on me at all times.

Joan of Arc suffered from premature boldness.

Bald or balding men, like myself, are disturbing because there is no definite end of the face.

He used to work on a Scandinavian gay porn site called "Norwegian Wood."

Somehow the sea knows a storm is coming, before the clouds gather, and before even the wind that brings them.

When life gives you lemons, make limoncello.

Definition of stupidity: approaching life primarily from the perspective of one's experience of it.

Partying is such sweet sorrow.

Do actual scabs — the ones on your body — use non-union skin cells?

Unclammy Valley™
A feminine hygiene spray for sex robots.

Mother Nietzsche.

I finally broke down and bought a Macbook Air for my upcoming travels. It is at once solicitous, condescending, and coercive...like a sexy kindergarten teacher.

I just had what I think must be technically the most boring dream of all time. I was waiting for an airport bus in a desolate outdoor suburban bus station somewhere in small-town Canada. When it finally arrived, the bus was full, and no-one could tell me when the next one would arrive. So I walked to a small mall a couple of miles away, and a boy I knew in primary school served me a tasteless Styrofoam cup of tea.
The end.

I love dogs, but I suspect their "loyalty" is over-rated. They usually don't seem to care which entity feeds them, pats them, takes them for walks, or throws them a ball. As long as someone does. Much like people.

Inter-medial question: Do Wes Anderson's 1990s movies qualify as the first Tumblr accounts?

Is an activist pacifist an oxymoron?

Isolations. Obliques. Elliptical.... The gym is so evasive!

"When a man gives a woman a book, he's trying to start a relationship. When a woman gives a man a book, she's trying to finish one."
(Merritt Symes)

"There is vice now, but you cannot be simply naughty."
(Elizabeth Bowen)

You know you're getting older when your wife refers to your private parts as "historic downtown."

So many unteachable moments.

I love being elsewhere, but hate travel.

Whoever said, "it's not the destination but the journey," clearly wasn't flying United.

Most of us live on a combination of revenue trickles.

AFTER THE REVOLUTION,
THESE WILL BE THE NEW CABINET POSTS

- Minister for Media Ecology
- Minister for Unalienated Labor
- Minister for Infrastructure and Serendipity
- Minister for Nonhuman Comrades
- Minister for Urban Pleasure Gardens and Car-Free Roads
- Minister of Defenses Down
- Minister for Transports Most Affecting
- Minister for Alcohol, Tobogganing, and Fireworks
- Minister for Communication-as-Différance
- Minister for Great Sex
- Minister for Foreign Affairs and Local Dalliances
- Minister for Spontaneous Tangos
- Minister for Organic Intellectuals
- Minister for Poetic Justice
- Minister for Sporting Chances
- Minister for Relocating Emotional Baggage
- Minister for the Scientific Arts
- Minister for Chillaxing
- Minister for Travels in Hyperreality
- Minister for Thought-Provoking Diversions
- Minister for Pointless Exercises
- Secretary of Health
- Chief Secretary to the Treasure Islanders
- Director of Orgone Energy
- Shadow Minister for Shadows, Silhouettes, and Other Tricks of the Light

The social contract, undermined by social contacts.

Are you really angry? Or are you just using this as an opportunity to indulge in the micro-*jouissance* of resentment?

Most people are repulsed by amorality more than immorality, since the latter at least uses morality as its polarized reference point. With amorality, all bets are off.

La vie sans frisson est dur.

There is no meaning of life. But there is meaning *for* life.

Today's oxymoron: fancy plane.

Today's tautology: involuntary memory.

Another oxymoron: right decision.

If newspapers were completely blank, they would be more edifying.

Spare a thought for the foolish angels, rushing in to places where they also fear to tread.

The cosmos silently hollers, "Can I get a witness?"

And the lifetime achievement award for comedy goes to both physics and gravity.

Frogs and cicadas = nature's Muzak.

Afterbirth: a bloody unpleasant thing that lasts around 70 years in most cases.

The love triangle found itself in a vicious circle while in the town square.

JUDGE: What is your profession?
BRODSKY: Poet. Poet and translator.
JUDGE: Who said you were a poet? Who assigned you that rank?
BRODSKY: No-one. Who assigned me to the human race?

The deserter berserker requested the mazurka.

Whenever a living system is sufficiently sophisticated or complex, sarcasm is bound to result (in the same way that carbon monoxide is bound to exude from certain organisms).

Kissing is a gateway drug.

This country has seen an increase of syringe-wielding maniacs demanding large amounts of money. The police refer to them as "doctors."

The YK2 problem: suffered by those who have already climbed Everest and see no point in scaling the world's second highest mountain.

"[John Waters] walked out of his Baltimore house and hitch-hiked to his apartment in San Francisco, over nine days with 21 rides, out of which has come the book CARSICK. Before he left, he wrote two novellas about it, one imagining the worst rides he might get and one imagining the best. His assistant read them and told him she could not tell the difference."

I just stepped into the same river. Twice!

Little known fact: long before the straw that broke the camel's back came the one that broke its spirit.

Diminishing returns of the eternal return.

The fetishism of minor similarities.

Will helicopter parents turn into drone grandparents?

What if swine really *love* pearls?

The older you get, the more you get to ride on the Inflammation Superhighway.

The generic clothing of middle-aged men practically scream out to the world: "What part of no more hot sex ever do you NOT find terrifying?"

Commutiny!

I intend to sue this hotel over its "Infinity Pool," for false advertising.

They say time marches on. But time is better considered a waltz.

Idea for graphic novel:
Dogs are actually alien spies, deep undercover, observing humans up close. At night they communicate with each other via walkie-talkies.

The TV remote is cruel optimism crystallized in plastic.

All the best or most important conversations happen in a parked car.

I was so annoying on the phone today that a telemarketer hung up on me.

Humans are basically the Australians of the galaxy.

The prostrate apostate potentate had an enlarged … appendix.

The unspoken question that hung over all gatherings of our teenage years: who will put what where and in who?"

If you have to "curate" your life, then you don't have one.

The pathetic phallusy.

The philosopher ponders his sex life:
"Why is there nothing and not something?"

Lonely phone booth by the river. Dislodges ancient memory. The fateful day I spent my 20-cent pocket money not on "a bag of mixed lollies" like usual, but a phone call to a girl from my school. I can still hear her green eyes through the receiver.

The yoghurt of human unkindness.

Maslow's lesser known Hierarchy of Occasional Whims.

We have reached the point where *Idiocracy* should be viewed as neo-realism.

These days, when the cat's away, the mice punch the clock and work diligently anyway.

The uncited. The bibliographically blind.

Even though they often passionately locked pupils, they rarely saw eye to eye.

Manic pixie girls taking elfies.

What if Magritte was really bad at drawing, and his famous *Treachery of Images* was actually an attempt to render a boat? Hence the clarifying caption, *Ceci, n'est pas une pipe*.

"If *I* don't take myself seriously, then who will?"
#wrongattitude

I bet Pablo Picasso *was* called an asshole. And on more than one occasion.

I h(e)a(r)t(e) New York.

Does anything sicken quicker than emotional pragmatism?

New York City = the Isle of the Glamorously Damned.

"We must find rhythms of self-care."
(Judith Butler, at Helen Tartar's funeral)

Love needs a circuit to exist. It's about conductivity; the crackle between hearts, minds, bodies, souls. If one person feels it for another, but the latter is unaware or cannot feel any wattage, then it might as well not exist.

If you weren't a tangible conduit to fleeting erotic metaphysical perfection I would barely give you the time of day.

Twilight of the Idols vs. the Idols of *Twilight*.

The secret to a good marriage is bi-annual performance reviews.

I like my panic like I like my stockings: sheer.

Judeo-Christian parents:
"I made you in my image; so you are forever in my debt."

Pagan children:
"You summoned me here without my permission, so this better be good!"

How is humanity supposed to figure out climate change or economic inequality when it can't even figure out the Reply All button?

People like to tell us that we "only use 5% of our brains." But can't the same be said for our bodies?

Boner Fide = an erection without the aid of Viagra.

Today's porn star name: Soaky Nutrients.

One day I would like to be Director of the Center for Things That Cannot Hold.

The sprites of hell wear Lululemon.

Old Russian saying:
"It's better to be healthy and rich than sick and poor."

The only pertinent ontological question when encountering art — or indeed life — is "to what extent am I interfacing with intelligence." (Understanding that both ethics and beauty are aspects of intelligence.)

And on the seventh day God declared: "Thou shalt travel all over the city looking at Open Houses. For I built this world, and want to flip it for a good price."

I didn't go to a rock show last night because you're only old once.

If you zoom in close, it's actually penises in little helmets all the way down.

Neoliberalism: "Think of your mouth as a smile-delivery system."

So when the 1% threaten to "leave the country," if they are faced with high taxes...isn't that like Ebola saying: "you be nice to me — or I'll stop liquefying your organs for good!"

Scientists have found a way to clone George Michael and Andrew Ridgeley. They call it a Double Whammy.

Subcategories of the male gaze: the male appraisal, the male leer, the male glance, the male ogle, etc.

Flattery will get you neither everywhere nor nowhere.
It might, however, get you about 41% of the way there.

I propose a national Generous Lover Database, to counterbalance the negativity of the Sex Offender Registry.

Life is fine, as long as you don't want anything from it.

Analogy, or the study of butts.

Q: What do you call ideological smut?
A: Impropaganda.

The tyranny of proximity.

Does facial recognition software fall in love with certain captured parameters?

Would you rather someone say to you, "I love you" or "fuck me!"? The latter signals an actual recognition of exchange, and an actual commitment — the commitment to be fucked — no matter how fleeting. To love someone and announce it to them is to dwell in Goethe's solipsism: "Just because I love you, what business is that of yours?"

Do I like Katy Perry? I don't know. Do you like toxic pink industrial meat slime?

If I said you were a toxic, treacherous, cold-hearted sea cow, would you hold it against me?

If The Clash were around today, would their big hit be called "London Texting"?

The best proof I have of the subconscious is the way I find myself humming some seemingly random and half-forgotten song, plucked from the Wurlitzer of my distant past; the lyrics for which perfectly capture my current conscious thoughts.

With its tentative forays, violent mood swings, and almost limitless sense of possibility, Spring is definitely the adolescent season.

Time puts all babies in the corner.

Where angels fear to tread...but love to cha-cha.

For the French theorist, it is not a case of—"It takes two to tango"—but rather, "The tango creates the virtual conditions in which the compossibility of the dyad emerges in dynamic actuality."

Q: What do you call it when the hangman is wearing flip-flops and a Hawaiian shirt?
A: A summery execution.

Reception theory would be more interesting if it was about weddings.

As reassuring as a tree's to-do list.

TEN BOOKS
THAT HAVE NOT AT ALL STAYED WITH ME

1 Any Murakami written after 1988

2 That one with the cloned school kids in cardigans who talk proper

3 Ummmm, I think there was a pirate. Or was it a knight?

4 Something about a tiger and . . . another tiger? Or was it a monkey?

5 Anything by Alain de Botton

6 Blink, or Clomp, or Stomp, or some piece of crap

7 That one with the yellow cover. You remember?

8 The one about the psychopath hurting the ladies. (In fact, all of the ones about the psychopaths hurting the ladies.)

9 The Unbearable Triteness of Something or Other

10 The Bible

"Are you coming to the Morris Dancing competition?"
"I'll be there with bells on."

How do I clear the cache of this memory foam mattress?

I have nothing to say. And I refuse to say it.

It's a shame about reification.

Why do I (still) know that the guy from The Lemonheads is Evan Dando? What useless information. And what a waste of memory space. If only I could swap out these cells for something potentially useful, like traffic patterns in Antwerp, or twelfth-century Persian love poems.

Day-dreams? I prefer dusk dreams.

Mistaken identity politics.

If I can't revolt, I don't want to join your dance.

"Identity" is the name we give to what an animal does with anger, fear, and desire.

The audible paintings of Georgia O'Kweef.

The original word for "pet" in Middle English loosely translates as: "*You* love me, don't you.... Yes you do!"

Alain Badiou — Event Planner.

Sometimes, in order to preserve something precious, it is necessary to abandon it.

Is there anything uglier than an attractive person demonstrably and unashamedly in love with someone other than you?

Lightning is just God taking selfies.

These dogs are like restless leg syndrome. But in dog form.

These days, it's not so much a case of "You get what you pay for," but "you pay for what you get."

The only problem with Yelp or TripAdvisor is that people are stupid, and always wrong.

The Apple logo is a sly acknowledgment that their ethos and business model are a sin.

I had a dream last night that we couldn't start our department meeting until we had sat through an awkward 10-minute live-action commercial by the university's new sponsors.

Now I'm staying in Brooklyn, Manhattan is literally a bridge too far.

One Direction: less the name of a boyband, and more the motto of Capital itself.

Shouldn't all mothers be arrested while giving birth, for "endangering the welfare of a child"? After all, what could be more dangerous than wrenching someone into existence?!

If less is more, then nothing is the most.

A somber chain of restaurants called OCIM — Oh Crap It's Monday.

I love the smell of learning outcomes in the morning.

If you are really worried about speaking too soon, you would never speak at all.

After my dream last night — in which I had to give a lecture on a topic I couldn't remember anything about — a window pops up:
"You may also enjoy:
—Trying to carry 16 suitcases from a train, before it leaves the station.
—Trying to find a good place to urinate inside a very busy, labyrinthine hotel.
—Trying to find somewhere for a romantic assignation with that woman from the insurance commercial.
—Flying majestically like a condor over the Andes, until your arms get tired, and you can only flap about 2 feet off the ground, before slamming into a fire hydrant."

A women's fencing team called: "Ladies who Lunge."

In the age of Snapchat and Instagram, will our "private parts" soon be known as our "now out in public parts"?

The worst thing about social injustice — besides the injustice itself, of course — is that it turns us all into handwringing whiny boars. How to respond to injustice while also maintaining a *joie de vivre*? That is the impossible question.

Opium: the religion of the select few.

A naked bottom is a virtual spanking.

Walk like a callipygian.

If corporations really were people, then they'd be called Blaine, and have bad plastic surgery, and smile falsely at you while saying upbeat things like, "uh huh," and "I hear ya, buddy" — all while furiously rifling through your pockets, before turning you upside down and shaking the change that might be hidden in your ears.

Capitalism *is* the global financial crisis.

Meteorologists admit that they made the whole "silver lining" thing up.

I haven't made a single mistake in my life. I've just made a lot of good decisions that went really badly.

I'm feeling vaguely regruntled about things.

After a certain age, one is grateful to reach Cloud Four or Five.

At least five reliable eateries have closed around my office in the last couple of months due to skyrocketing rents. Soon enough there will be no food places left. So the local workers better figure out how to get nutrients from Coach bags and Zara slacks pronto, or they are all going to die out.

That one time Molly Bloom had a secret date with a Scrivener, and the next day they both replied "maybe" to everything.

To a nail, everything looks like a hammer.

Why do people seem incapable of mentioning *La Jetée* without immediately noting that it was "the inspiration for Terry Gilliam's *12 Monkeys*"? This is like feeling obliged to mention *Game of Thrones* whenever one references Icelandic sagas.

If we take Burroughs at his word, to study language is to become a virologist.

"A nanny? It's like a dog walker for humans."

Who you are has almost nothing to do with your personality.

Summa Cum Laude Than Others.

Families are all cases of Stockholm Syndrome.

If there is a God, then He's a lot like Woody Allen. Moody, manic, melancholic, and morally dubious. Did some great things back in the day, but is now stuck on autopilot. Indeed, everything He has produced for ages is basically self-indulgent geriatric-infantile pap. And yet almost no-one turns down the "opportunity" to appear in it.

I used to wake up at 4.30 AM every morning, to milk my mind for thoughts about the previous day, and scribble them down in a little black book. This was when I was working on a diary farm.

Your delusional coping mechanism isn't as good as my delusional coping mechanism.

Being "beloved" is all well and good. But what we all crave, above all, is to be *desired*.
(cf. Robin Williams)

The only problem with New York City is that it's actively trying to kill all its inhabitants.

The sweet duet of jackhammers both inside and outside the building.

Humans are essentially the baby boomers of the animal kingdom. There are a lot of good ones, but as a whole, we basically ruined the world.

"Sydney" is an aboriginal word for "babyccino."

Even harder than speaking truth to power? Speaking truth to liberals.

Much as I hate Starbucks, I have to admit they have an original business plan. Public toilets, with coffee.

Labor Day pseudo-haiku:

> *Downtown in Summer*
> *Many bizarre body shapes*
> *Like Star Wars cantina*

Short story idea: Like Saramago's *Blindness*, but everyone wakes up, unable to make small talk or pointless conversation. Every now and again you will hear a philosophical discourse or lover's confession, but mostly the entire city is silent. Certainly phones are now useless.

I love surreptitiously watching other people surreptitiously watching other people.

I don't know if you've noticed, but there are some amazing-looking people in New York.

My dreams are well cast, well lit, and reasonably well edited. However, they are badly written and directed.

MTA announcement:
"Because of deconstruction, no subways are running outside the text."

Flint Michigan. If you can make it here, you can make it *anywhere*.

Is it just me, or does the recorded voice on the phone suddenly become passive aggressive when I ask to speak to a (human) representative?

When you are 20 you know nothing. When you are 40 you also know nothing. But at least you *know* you know nothing.

Pro-tip: don't watch *Rosemary's Baby* after just moving into a co-op building on the Upper West Side.

Stripper name: "Dusty Archives."

New dish made from ingredients gleaned from Central Park: "Ramble bramble scramble."

Being serious is not the same as taking oneself seriously.

Nothing gets my pulse racing like the phrase "complimentary webinar."

In my dream last night I received an email that said, "we presume you will now all be halfwits, since we no longer have the money for fullwits."

Digital Heraclitus:
"You can never stream the same dubstep file twice."

Chickens. I count them not.

ME: "So who can tell me what 'taxonomy' means?"
STUDENTS: [*long silence*]
ME: "Think of the Natural History Museum."
STUDENT: "Oh. Is it like when you stuff a dead animal?"

That morsel of contempt which we all subconsciously reserve for anyone and everyone who falls in love with somebody other than ourselves.

The 1956 version of *Invasion of the Body Snatchers* was about communism and ideological indoctrination. The 1978 version was about neo-liberalism and rampant gentrification.

I predict that next year's fitness craze will be power-sauntering.

New message from HR:
"Don't forget: next Thursday is Bring your Illegitimate Love-Child to Work Day."

"A dime for your thoughts." #inflation

I seem to be watching a gluten-free spaghetti Western.

I'd like to open a bakery that doesn't actually sell anything. It would be called *Sweet Nothings*.

Tired of discussing difficult abstract questions about life, art, and society to professional, licensed thinkers? Introducing "Nous"—a new app that allows you to summon a local freelance philosopher or theorist, 24/7. Think of it as Uber for high conceptualists. Our digital map will show you which coffee shops, bars, and park benches our Nous participants are currently pontificating in or on; ready to be deployed to your vicinity at a moments notice.

(Also available, NousX, if you are in Brooklyn, and prefer your critical analysis via reasonably priced grad students.)

Last night I had a dream that Kim Dotcom was co-writing a book with my mother, called *Gendering the Algorithm*.

Some people are in show-business. Academics are in tell-business.

PSA:

A reminder that the tote bag population has exploded in recent years, in proportion to the increase in hipster-nerds in the area. Tote bags prefer to affix themselves to aging hippies and young, English majors, around the shoulder area. (Disease vectors include NPR, the *New Yorker*, and—more recently—*n+1*.) Don't forget to check for tote bags every evening before going to bed, for while they are large and visible, they can be taken for granted, and mistakenly considered harmless. Tote bags can carry all sorts of parasites, including the dreaded Liberal Disease, which can lead to reading Zadie Smith or living in Vermont.

MEMO

From: The King
To: All the King's Men
CC: All the King's Horses
Re: Ovum Training Course

Please remember there will be an information session today about Emergency Egg Reconstruction (EER) tools and techniques. The location is the other side of the wall. Coffee and cookies will be provided.

Woodpecker — the world's only one-word redundant phrase?

The tristesse of the trystless.

Having a cast-iron pan is as close as I'll likely get to the time and responsibility of having a kid.

"In 1980, Yourcenar was the first female member elected to the Académie française. An anecdote tells of how the bathroom labels were then changed in this male-dominated institution: 'Messieurs | Marguerite Yourcenar.'"

Breaking news:
Scientists confirm that "the sighs of lovers" contribute to global warming more than carbon emissions.

The neighborhood drunk is locally sauced.

You've gotta fight for your right to pâté.

My childhood was a seamless combination of *Gummo* and *My Dinner with Andre*.

Extreme Pickling magazine.

Q: What do you call the guy who takes care of the large maze in the garden?
A: A hedge fun manager.

I don't regret *too* many moments in the classroom, thankfully. But I *do* wish I hadn't instinctively made those hip movements, while quoting Nine Inch Nails' "Closer" the other day.

Yet another sign I'm not a millennial. I try to say goodbye at the end of a chat session, rather than simply stop.

What comes after millennials? Minecrafters, maybe?

The hot nanny went to the hootenanny at the ol' tannery.

Kim Kardashian = the most photographed barn in America.

I have reached the age where doing a number 2 is quicker than a number 1.

No matter how much money you have, you always feel like you have around half the amount you actually need.

Outsourcerer.

Liv Tyler + Admiral Ackbar = Megan Draper.

My two favorite imaginary punk bands:
Sweat Mustache
Brunch Vomit

I wonder what happens when a euphemism meets an innuendo.

TL;DR
(Too Lame; Didn't Read)

New slogan:
"New York City: Let's hope that's dog poop."

New slogan 2:
"New York City: Let's hope that's air-conditioner sprinkle."

In any given jazz band, it's always the saxophonist who has sex oftenist.

It's a little-known fact that Oregon is so called after the great Oregano Rush of 1839.

Everyone has "sexual needs." Everyone!
   That means not only you, but your parents, your children, your siblings, your grandparents, your uncles and aunts; as well as your teacher, your neighbor, your dentist, your chiropodist, your accountant, your dog walker, your ombudsmen, your local council representative. That guy next to you in the elevator. That woman who just made your coffee.
   Everyone.
   I know! Gross, right?

I know I'm not the first to make this connection, but from the perspective of the present, it really does seem like *Space Invaders* was invented and introduced to train a new generation in answering an endless avalanche of emails.

Is there anything less sexy than an ad for lingerie?

Žižek is always "willing to go to the end," because — like a good Hegelian — he believes there is an end.

To "behave" is to combine the two most fundamental forms of being, or verbal modes—*to be* and *to have*. To "misbehave" is thus to *be* in the wrong, and to *possess* oneself improperly.

There is a parasite that can burrow into an insect's brain, and then make it do its bidding, as if it were riding the poor infested creature like a horse—both physically and mentally. We also have such a parasite. It's called ideology.

First rule of Publishing Club: Don't write a book with someone whose last name comes before you in the alphabet.

In my dream last night, an earnest archaeologist explained to me that "the record is clear: windows were invented two centuries before doors."

As a child, my biggest moment of sheer shock and disbelief— besides learning that we all are destined to die—was being told that I couldn't go and live in any country I wanted.

If you definitely don't want a magazine to be read, then put it in the magazine rack.

Humble pie? Or chagrin gratin?

Why is there a "heat wave" and a "cold snap"? Can't waves be cold?

When someone says: "You've got your work cut out for you," they mean you have a great deal to do. But the phrase itself sounds like half the work has already been done by someone else.

I wish I had learned Chinese and Spanish. Then I could speak to approximately 80% of the world's people.

So far, being a dean is a lot like *The Knick*. Except my secret drawer is full of chocolate, rather than cocaine.

Alien: "Take me to your anarcho-syndicalist representative governmental body."

Let's not forget that Jean-Luc Nancy wrote a 100-page article that could be boiled down to saying, "boobs are awesome."

I wonder what would shock a Victorian time-traveler more about the present day. That people walk down the street essentially naked? Or that they do so while having a conversation with someone who is not actually there.

The exploitation of extinction:
A reality TV competition which pits two endangered species against each other. Two teams, representing their respective totem animals, compete to win the prize: enough funding from UNESCO to buy the winning species a few more years away from poachers and/or starvation. The loser is left to perish in a bittersweet montage.

Q: Who is the most paranoid woman in Russia?
A: Natasha Izzy-Ovenoff.

My work day is much easier to cope with if I pretend I'm trapped inside a long-running telenovela.

Is it possible to get more cultural capital on credit?

"Ebony and Ivory" is a heart-warming song about human harmony. But it conveniently forgets that the piano only exists because of the destruction of forests and slaughter of elephants!

Odor is noise for the nose.

People can forgive you anything, except being happy.

New York City is pure noise, extruded into a bewildering variety of material forms.

WINE-SHOP GUY: "Are you having a party?"
ME: "No."

For the most part, the Theory blogosphere is a global textile sweatshop for the Emperor's new clothes.

This Halloween I'm going as a slutty divisional curriculum standards subcommittee member.

When I was a kid I'd tell people that my father was a cross-dresser... because he'd always yell at me while buttoning up his shirt.

My new totem is the New York City water tower.

Saturn Photoshops his children.

Is there a sadder artifact in this world than a curriculum vitae? No matter how accomplished, it says nothing about the person whose name is at the top.

The Upper West Side suddenly seems way cooler if I pretend everyone is normcore.

That sense of dread when an academic says that their public remarks will be *relatively* brief.

Why did I decide to go into academia? Mostly the glamor.

Occupation: wheel-reinventor.

Life: An Abuser's Manual.

Funny to think how different film theory might have been if Hitchcock hadn't been raised by an aloof, ambiguously gendered, quasi-Nazi.

America's complicated relationship with personal boundaries and consent goes all the way back to the Fondling Fathers.

To eat at a half-decent restaurant in New York City is to be robbed at fork-and-knife-point.

Most people know that William Gibson wrote his prophetic future-noir classic *Neuromancer* on a typewriter. Less people are aware that Emily Brontë wrote *Wuthering Heights* on a steam-powered Jacquard Loom.

"'Emotional support pig' kicked off plane after becoming disruptive." Before reading the article, I assumed this headline was referring to somebody's husband.

Thanksgiving is the day that most American households ritually slaughter a feathered creature in order to placate the angry gods of family and nation.

I exaggerate more than anyone else in the world.

It was around this time of year, when I was ten years old, that my father took me to the Christmas Spectacular at Radio City Hall. He enticed me there with promises of the Rockettes, who he explained — with a gleam in his eye — were dancing ladies famous for standing in a line and kicking their legs up in the air in unison. However, the Rockettes chose this year to debut an avant-garde alternative, dressed as toy soldiers, making strange androgynous mechanical movements, with nary a kick or a shimmy. I wept with bitter disappointment for the rest of the show, and have been suspicious of experimental performance art ever since.

Pity the poor bedroom chair. No matter how fancy or lushly upholstered—and no matter how forcefully it features in reveries of sun-dappled daydreams of autumn afternoon reading sessions—it will forever be buried under an improvised and ad hoc drapery of underwear, overwear, and assorted clothing; each creasefully awaiting its belated return to a designated drawer or wardrobe. In the meantime the chair mutely endures its all-too-predictable indignity, smothered and barely visible.

A student just wrote to me at 3 AM to say that they stumbled back upon a note they wrote, quoting me in class: "You are an excretion of cosmic desire."

15 Things You Should Stop Doing, Now You're In Your 20s/30s/40s/50s/60s:
#1. Stop reading bullshit listicles online.

When anyone finishes a sentence with, "…because of the economy," politely correct them. "Oh, you mean because of the deliberate, systemic, relentless planet-destroying, hope-crushing austerity machine, engineered for the obscene ransacking of the commons by the never-rich-enough parasite class, in which government, legislature, industry, black markets, and mainstream media are cozily complicit; buttressed by the careful monopolization and militarization of violence, as well as the strategically deployed, cynically empty, promises of somehow possibly being a vanishingly anomalous exception to the rule of accelerated impoverishment via the cold and capricious gonk-machine-claw of success?"

TO THE TUNE OF LCD SOUNDSYSTEM'S
"I'M LOSING MY EDGE"

The kids are coming up from behind.
But I was there.
I was there when Kojève lectured on Hegel to Bataille.
I was there when Bataille tried to sacrifice that guy in the Paris sewers.
I was there when that other guy poured water over Lacan's head.
I was there when Cioran lit de Beauvoir's first cigarette in the Café de Flore.
I was there when Deleuze gave his last lecture to a nurse before jumping out the window.
I was there when Foucault dissed Chomsky on live Dutch TV.
I was there when Kristeva spoke for two hours to the waiter about the gross skin on her hot chocolate.
I was there when Angela Davis raised her fist in the Embassy Auditorium.
I was there when Lingis howled, dressed in only gold paint, in the dark, with a flashlight.
I was there when Spivak stubbed out a cigarette in the palm of her hand before taking the podium.
I was there when Baudrillard left the room so the translator could answer the questions.
I was there when Stiegler spoke in court after robbing a bank.
I was there when Graham Harman answered an email, saying "yes, I'll come to your conference."
I was there when Reza emerged from the Iranian oilfields to channel his Cyclonopedia.
I was there when Thacker confronted Glenn Beck on Meet the Press.
But I'm losing my edge.
The kids are coming up from behind.
But I was there.

The lovers' bed is a negotiation of knees, as much as an accommodation of needs.

Negentropy walks into a bar…and then diffuses throughout the space.

Negentropy—the self-delusional, cocky young punk of the space-time continuum.

And this is how the world ends—not with a bang, but with the anemic croon of Bon Iver through the neighbor's wall.

After a good Turkish meal, we gather closer round the table for a post-hummus tale.

12th century: Wine, women, and song.
18th century: Libations, labia, and librettos.
1920s: Cocktails, coquettes, and chorales.
1960: Sex, drugs, and rock-and-roll.
2014: Adderall, avatars, and Auto-Tune.
     (or Vine, Viagra, and vocaloids)

I know why the caged bird has a Netflix subscription.

Academia comes from a Greek verb, meaning "to reward pomposity."

Only 20% of people who say "whatever!" actually mean *whatever*.

You haven't really lived until your heart starts beating.

Academia: Where being told "you write well" is meant as a warning, or an insult.

Badiou's four key "conditions" are art, love, politics, and science. Mine would probably be intelligence, beauty, enigma, and *frisson*.
...oh, and wine.

"Read it? I haven't even taught it!"
(anon.)

Humans will be the first species to grow a third articulated limb for the sole purpose of taking selfies.

The vulgar Western distillation of Buddhism is a philosophy espousing the wisdom of "no attachments." But that sounds suspiciously like Ayn Rand. Better to cultivate "*only* attachments," so that there is no self beyond the organization and appreciation of one's valences. Rather than a strong self, free of others, there is a knotting of selves. Then, searing grief will be ever entwined with nourishing joy.

Wall St. + Madison Avenue = the doucheoisie.

Why did Weird Al Yankovic never do a parody song about a highbrow removalist company called "Move a Bust"?

I'm still waiting for "gormcore," where people dress like Flay, Fuchsia, Swelter, Prunesquallor, and Steerpike from Mervyn Peake's *Gormenghast*.

There are in fact only two fundamental emotions or motivations: "Look at me!" and "Don't look at me!"

Sometimes, for no apparent reason, my inner voice slips into sounding exactly like Daisy from *Downton Abbey*.

Shipping routes were the original pier-to-pier network.

"Perishables" is probably the biggest subset in the universe. Or, from a different angle, the smallest.

What's it like to be a battery?

You can't build an ivory tower without doing a lot of poaching.

I wanna fuck you like a technocrat!

The most important part of a love letter is punctuation. And few things have more aphrodisiacal power than the right syntax for the moment.

Lacan had a name for the selfie stick, *avant la lettre*: "the phallus."

Your house or apartment is your IRL address.

Character name: April May Joon.

If you want to work on your glutes, you go to the gym. But what if you want to work on your gravitas?

Our desires are what connect us to, and alienate us from, each other.

Is fondness inherently condescending?

Early Modern headline:
"Low quality yarn leads to looming crisis."

It's no coincidence that the notion of "terroir" is born the very moment that specific local space becomes an endangered species.

Art project:
Sexual harassment/sensitivity training course online, for people who feel they have been harassed by succubi and other spirits from the netherworld.

The only way I would consider watching the Grammys is if they were an award show to honor the best grandmothers.

Must I take it to the next level? What if I'm perfectly happy at the level I'm at?

My wife puts more time and thought into choosing a rug than she did a husband.

Short story about someone being spammed by an old account of a dead friend or colleague. The presumption is that the account has been hacked to sell knock-off meds. But it turns out that limbo is even worse than we thought, and after death, we are all obliged to do direct digital marketing for several eons, until heaven or hell free up some space.

When I grow up, I'd like to be head of the Feral Reserve.

I have accomplished many things. But becoming a grown-up isn't one of them.

The Great Nap is Dead!

Colleagues. The community of those who have one thing in common.

Four incommensurable satisfactions / accomplishments:
1) mastering a genre (Lubitsch, Ford, Kurosawa, etc.)
2) reinventing a genre (Welles, Hitchcock, Kubrick, etc.)
3) inventing a new genre (Tati, Cassavetes, Marker, etc.)
4) going beyond genre altogether (Varda, Tarkovsky, Jodorowsky, etc.)

The latest white privilege: complaining about white people, while being white.

The more fast-paced this world becomes, the longer it takes to get anything done.

Clearly the MTA isn't really about public transport. It's more likely an experiment in keeping a wildly diverse city from boiling over, by giving everyone a common enemy.

Uncanny valley girl.

Ah February. You truly are the calendar's kidney stone.

Uber, UKIP, Ubik.

LITERARY FACEBOOK FEED

› **Mallarmé** just wished **Apollinaire** a happy birthday.

› **Ezra Pound** just poked **Samuel Beckett**.

› **Robert Walser** just posted two indecipherable images to his album, "microscripts."

› **Simone de Beauvoir** just changed her relationship to "It's complicated."

› **Marcel Proust** just posted a selfie. #wholedayinbed #stillmoreproductivethanyou

› **James Joyce** update: "Crowd-sourcing time. Who can remember the lyrics to the title song from Martha? I'm trying to work it in the Sirens section I'm struggling with at the moment. Must finish by Friday, though. Would rather be eating SNACKS tho. LOL."

› **Simone Weil**: "Does anyone happen to have a pdf of **Hildegard von Bingen**'s Scivias?"

› **F. Scott Fitzgerald** just unfriended **Ernest Hemmingway**.

› **Virginia Woolf** just invited you to her book-launch. Will you attend? Yes? Maybe?

› **George Orwell** just invited you to play Animal Farmville.

› **Ayn Rand** just asked you to sign the petition against Charity of All Stripes.

You can determine a person's age by how much they care about birds.

I definitely have a type. And God am I bored of it!

What if our thoughts are broadcast from Elsewhere? Schizophrenics are then cases where the wires get crossed, so several mind-voices occur on one line.

Any sense of spirituality I feel depends absolutely on the absence of a supreme being. Creation is only miraculous insofar as there is no Creator.

The interminable length of most *New Yorker* pieces makes much more sense to me, now I know that the author gets $2 a word.

Skype needs to add a filter so it looks like you're smartly dressed when really wearing pajamas.

Due to inflation, a picture is now worth 1,854 words.

A pickle store called *Life of Brine*.

If you listen very carefully, you can hear the bears hitting the snooze button, not yet ready to end the sweet lethargy of their hibernation.

Q: Where does Jack Frost keep his savings?
A: In a snow bank.

Q: What does Jack Frost use to call his snow bank manager?
A: A snowmobile.

I just realized that Meatloaf's amorous point of exception ("I would do anything for love, but I won't do that") was already foreshadowed by Hall & Oates ("I'll do almost anything, That you want me to do, But I can't go for that...No can do").

America: where they charge your credit card to take your fingerprints.

Some will tell you that it's safer in New York than 20 years ago, because you can walk around with very little chance of getting mugged or robbed. But tourists and citizens are still being robbed blind. It's now just called "the check," "the bill," or "the rent."

Sometimes you just have to eat a fuckload of gluten.

Nothing could be less my motto than "I will sleep when I'm dead."

The pessimist credo: If life gives you lemonade, then reverse engineer it into lemons.

We never truly forgive those who make, or allow us to, fall in love with them.

We need a Bechdel test for capitalism. If someone speaks to you about nothing but shopping, gadgets, celebrities, trends, entertainment products, temporal industrial objects, curated experiences, personal performance, etc., then they fail.

They say if life gives you lemons, then make lemonade. But what if life gives you kumquats?

Austerity tip #34:
Postpone Christmas till the first week of January. Then you can find a perfectly good "pre-loved" Christmas tree on the sidewalk, for free!

I have a truth ache.

Is it wrong to consider suicide because there seems little point in living in a world where tomatoes have completely lost their flavor?

In Central Park this afternoon, I saw a man lift up his rather large dog over his head, so that the pooch could enjoy the fantasy of being possibly able to catch the squirrel that taunted it from a branch several feet above its head. I immediately thought: this is love. One creature helping another feel stronger than it actually is for a few exciting seconds.

It's taken me over forty years to truly appreciate Rimbaud's famous words, *Je est un autre* ("I am an other," or, more literally, "I is an other"). The self truly is another, who just happens, by virtue of cosmic contingency, to be currently under one's existential—and physical—stewardship. Each individual should be as responsible to their self, as they are to another (or to The Other, as Continental philosophers like to say). This is not to flirt with Ayn Rand or any other self-centric paradigm. Rather, it is to *literally* incorporate Levinas, who insisted we prioritize our neighbors' needs over our own. But we are also our own neighbor; forced to take up residence in this body, and succumb to auto-hospitality. And so, recognize the other-within-the-self. And look after that person. So that this person may look after others more effectively and compassionately.

You lost me at hello.

APPENDIX 1
GLOSSARY

ANGRICAN (*n.*) — the kind of churchgoer who flies off into a rage at the sight of single mothers.

BROKER (*n.*) — mediating profession so arrogant that it boasts of its own designs in its job title. That is, to make their clients less rich.

CLAPTRAP (*adj./n.*) — nineteenth-century slang for "prostitute."

COLUMNIST (*n.*) — particularly noxious form of JOURNALIST. "All columnists should be pulped and turned back into paper" (*Sabrina*).

CONFIDENCE (*n.*) — see DELUSION.

DELUSION (*n.*) — see PEOPLE.

EXPIREANCE (*n.*) — the experience of dying.

FLAPLING (*adj.*) — the gormless expression on a television presenter's face when their co-presenter is talking.

FUCKENNAYLIA (*n. pl.*) — a particularly Australian affirmation of a drunken, Dionysian party.

GLUNTING (*v.*) — the activity of impersonating the orgasmic noises of one's own boyfriend for the amusement of female friends (usually performed after two glasses of cheap champagne).

HEADERPHOBIA (*n.*) — the mental paralysis created in direct inverse ratio to the need to think of a subject heading for an email message.

IMMGRATE (*adj.*) — an immigrant who is not grateful enough to the host country for its hospitality (at least in the eyes of those who believe they constitute the host country).

INEPOTISM (*adj.*) — the process of appointing inept people to posts simply because they are known to the search committee. (See ACADEMIA.)

INFACTUATION (*n.*) — a true obsession.

INTEGRITY (*n.*) — what people pretend to believe in if they have no money.

JEWRY DUTY (*n.*) — the obligation to actively reflect on the many trials and tribulations of the sons and daughters of Abraham

KARAOKE (*n./v.*) — Japanese word for "hell".

KATOMETER (*n.*): One of the longest natural measurements in the known universe — the distance between a good Kate Bush song and a bad one.

LOCO-MOTIVE (*n.*) — a train of thought which leads to a crazy reason for doing something.

LOVE (*n./v.*) — see AKRASIA.

MELANCHOMMUNISM (*n.*) — a particularly dejected, nostalgic, and egalitarian form of political community.

MOANAD (*n.*) — whining and/or orgasmic singularity.

OZTRACISM (*n.*) — being forced or obliged to live in Australia.

PATHOS (*n.*) — see SEX.

PENULTIMATUM (*n.*) — the second last threat a scorned lover makes before leaving.

PLEISURE (*n.*) — the life-affirming feeling you get when not working.

PRECRASTINATION (*v.*) — all those little things you do before settling in to a day of avoiding things you should be doing.

READ (*v.*) — a dubious action, since it is the same in both the past and present tense, so you never really know if you've done it, or you're doing it.

REBUFF (*v.*) — to return to the gym after a prolonged absence.

REVAMP (*n.*) — a woman (or drag queen) of a certain age, who decides to start wearing black clothes and smudgy eye-makeup again.

SEX (*n.*) — the metaphysical attempt to confound physical laws; esp. the universal prohibition against two bodies inhabiting the same space. See also PATHOS.

SHORTING (*n.*) — to be content in the moment; a sense of plenitude or concord with the status quo. The opposite of LONGING.

SODOMETRO (*v.*): the term for when someone slams into your derrière at the Paris underground turnstiles in order to avoid paying for a ride.

SOPHISTICATION (*n.*) — the ability to eloquently articulate personal misery, combined with the inability to achieve any satisfaction from having done so.

STRATISFACTION (*n.*) — the pleasure which stems from being higher on the social ladder than somebody else.

SUFFOCATERER (*n.*) — person (traditionally a mother) who insists on cooking for and feeding their children, plus extended kinship networks, in a way which smothers them.

TESTEMOANIAL (*n.*) — the memory of the noise a man makes when somebody kicked him in the nuts.

TRIPIDATION (*n.*) — the sense of low-key dread that accompanies one while heading to the airport.

UNANIMOSITY (*n.*) — when everyone in the room hates you.

VINDICATION (*n.*) — the feeling of self-justification one gets after choosing, and drinking, the right bottle of wine.

WHORTICULTURE (*n.*) — the realization that, to quote *Withnail and I*, flowers are "merely prostitutes for the bees."

ZENOPHOBIA (*n.*) — the fear of hitting your target.

APPENDIX II
A TAXONOMY OF BRUISES

This short text has delighted, confused, and provoked scholars since its discovery in the Eastern Arabah archaeological digs, near the ancient city of Petra, in 1844. The dispute continues regarding precisely how to categorize such a work: an irony not lost on those representing all sides of the argument, given that the text itself is explicitly dedicated to the act of categorization. The original Latin script dates from the seventh century AD, was inscribed on the finest vellum (suggesting official patronage), remarkably well preserved in a garnet-encrusted bronze cylinder, seemingly designed for just this purpose. Liberal use of terms and phrases in Arabic suggest the work was written—probably collectively—between neo-Aristotelian theologians and Persians of the cosmopolitan Sufi persuasion. (Such collaborations were reasonably common, up until the Crusades.) Certain interweavings of monism, occasionalism, and other heterodoxia reinforce this hypothesis, given that no single religious or philosophical orientation can be definitively obtained (much as the experts try, from one perspective or another). The rather risky—not to mention risqué—topic of the flesh is clearly contextualized within a Christian sensibility, yet threatens to escape at any moment into the more sensual pages of The Song of Solomon,

---

This piece originally appeared in *Cabinet* magazine in slightly different form. We thank them for permission to include here.

or certain pseudo-Islamic homages to terrestrial pleasure. One aspect of this anomalous work, upon which the scholars do *agree, is the remarkable form of the taxonomy itself, anticipating the system usually attributed to Linnaeus himself. The elusive story surrounding the Father of Taxonomy's classificatory system—gestating behind his stern Swedish brow—and his knowledge or ignorance of the present text, has yet to be written. Such a coincidence, however, is most provocative, even to the casual student of the natural sciences and the history of ideas. In any case, this edition faithfully renders the original table of elements: itself a most suggestive sketch of that "significant ephemera" which should be of interest to the archaeologist and anthropologist, as much as to the physician and metaphysician. This scholastic exercise stands alone as a quiet murmur amongst our species' ongoing obsession with placing kind with kind, and separating goats from sheep, wheat from chaff, night from day, and love from less exalted types of attraction. If nothing else, in regard to the amateur reader, "A Taxonomy of Bruises"* (Partitio de Cicatricibus) *can form the basis of spirited discussion for one's next salon or tiresome train journey.*

—Dominic Pettman, Founding Editor-at-Large, The Institute of Incoherent Geography, 2010

PREAMBLE

It is said that both man and woman bruise "like a peach." And it is true that mortals share a kind of flesh with the succulent products of the fruit tree. Perhaps God — praise be His name — has prepared a secret affinity between our own bodies and the sweet texture yielded from a harvest of apricots, nectarines, peaches, pears, and plums. It is even possible that the apple — symbol and cause of Adam's exile from Paradise — forms an invisible continuity with the soft tissues of our Earthly bodies. (Strangely, the beasts do not seem to bruise, suggesting a closer kinship with certain botanical entities, at least in terms of the subject under examination.) Folk wisdom tells us that the fair sex bruise more easily than the male, and to this we must concur, with certain exceptions, detailed anon.

Those trained in the arts of Hippocrates will tell you that a bruise is caused not by a sharp object, nor a light one, but of a blunt and heavy disposition. The skin must not break or lacerate, but remain in plane, to act as cover for the local injury beneath, swelling and darkening black and purple, like a storm cloud trapped inside the body of young and old alike. (Unlike the peach, the bruises of men heal — or at least, the majority do, of those we have yet to inventory.) But here the physicians are indifferent and uncurious, content to treat one such contusion with another. The learned, however, who seek to learn ever anew, take a longer path, and offer this taxonomy of bruises as a gift to descendents of a similar spirit, to complete as they see fit.

BRUISES OF THE FIRST TYPE: DOMESTIC

cicatrix pedis: a bruise of the foot

cicatrix cruris: a bruise of the legs (lower)

cicatrix femoris: a bruise of the legs (upper)

cicatrix clunium: a bruise of the buttocks

cicatrix manus: a bruise of the hand

cicatrix bracchii: a bruise of the arms (lower)

cicatrix lacerti: a bruise of the arms (upper)

cicatrix pectoris: a bruise of the torso (front)

cicatrix tergi: a bruise of the torso (back)

cicatrix colli: a bruise of the neck

cicatrix faciei: a bruise of the face

cicatrix palmae: a bruise caused by an open hand

cicatrix pugni: a bruise caused by a closed fist

cicatrix ex inquisitione obscurata: a bruise caused by searching for an object in the dark

cicatrix domestica: a bruise caused by clumsiness, inflicted by tables, chairs, furniture, or doorframes *cicatrix ex gravi*: a bruise caused by dropping a heavy object

cicatrix nubilosa: a bruise resulting from daydreaming or slowness of mind

cicatrix ex casu: a bruise caused by falling (for instance, from a ladder)

cicatrix ex casu alieno: a bruise caused by accident, inflicted by another (for instance, an overzealous gesture)

cicatrix ex pecore: a bruise caused by one's livestock

cicatrix ex equitando: a bruise caused by the riding of a horse

cicatrix ex cinyphe: a bruise resulting from the bite of an insect

cicatrix religiosa: a bruise resulting from religious fervor or penance

cicatrix conjugis: a bruise caused by the hand of one's husband or wife, for being disagreeable

cicatrix parentis: a bruise caused by the hand on one's father or mother, for being disobedient

cicatrix avunculi: a bruise caused by one's uncle, for being lazy

cicatrix apud familiam: a bruise, self-inflicted, to garner sympathy within the family

cicatrix in familiam: a bruise, self-inflicted, to garner sympathy *regarding* one's family *cicatrix ex obliterato*: a bruise for which one can no longer remember the cause

cicatrix ex ignorato: a bruise for which one never was cognizant of the cause

cicatrix ex dyscolitate: a bruise resulting from ill humor

cicatrix ex ludo nimio: a bruise resulting from horse-play

cicatrix natalis: a bruise which peaks on the day of one's own birth

cicatrix naevia: a bruise which overlaps with a birthmark

cicatrix conpicta: a bruise wished away through the artful application of powders or paste

cicatrix mnemosyna: a bruise brought back from travels afar

cicatrix ad osculum patruelis: a bruise which invites the kiss of a cousin

cicatrix nuptialis: a bruise received on one's wedding night

cicatrix ex conplexu: a bruise resulting from an excessive embrace

cicatrix ex coitu: a bruise resulting from passionate love-making (within wedlock)

cicatrix ex fornicatione: a bruise resulting from passionate love-making (out of wedlock)

cicatrix ex masturbatione: a bruise acquired during onanistic activity, as divine punishment of the same *cicatrix patefaciens*: a bruise that betrays a secret

cicatrix zelotypa: a bruise stemming from jealousy

cicatrix libidinis: a bruise stemming from desire

cicatrix libidinis zelotypa: a bruise stemming from jealous desire

cicatrix latrini: a bruise stemming from a dispute over the latrine

BRUISES OF THE SECOND TYPE: CIVIC/PUBLIC

cicatrix ex pede suo: a bruise formed after tripping over one's own feet

cicatrix ex pede alieno: a bruise formed after tripping over the feet of another

cicatrix crystalli: a bruise which blossoms after slipping on ice

cicatrix musci: a bruise which forms after slipping on moss

cicatrix virgae: a bruise resulting from birch cane or willow paddle for misbehavior (especially in a convent or seminary)

cicatrix arboris: a bruise inflicted by the ground after falling from a tree

cicatrix muri: a bruise inflicted by the ground after falling from a wall

cicatrix fenestrae: a bruise caused by an object falling from a window

cicatrix plostri: a bruise caused by a cart, or other moving vehicle

cicatrix verpae: a bruise caused by dancing around the May Pole

cicatrix ex cubito concubitando: a bruise inflicted (most commonly in the vicinity of the rib cage) by a companion's elbow, deployed to draw attention to the proximity of a comely stranger

cicatrix ex calce submensali: a bruise received from a kick underneath the dinner table

cicatrix stulta: a bruise acquired while trying to draw attention to oneself in a vain, foolish manner

cicatrix crapulata: a bruise sustained while intoxicated

cicatrix Jovis: a bruise given as a poisoned gift by a rival for a woman's (or girl's) affections

cicatrix Jovis graeci: a bruise given as a poisoned gift by a rival for a man's (or boy's) affections

cicatrix monita: a bruise suffered as a warning of worse to come, unless certain conditions are met

cicatrix fata: a bruise suffered as a warning of worse to come, no matter how the sufferer comports him or herself in future

cicatrix nobilis: a bruise caused by one of noble birth

cicatrix plebis: a bruise caused by one of lower social rank

cicatrix nobilioris: a bruise resulting from (accidentally) bruising someone of higher social rank

cicatrix insidiarum: a bruise resulting from revolutionary or mutinous activity

cicatrix barbara: a bruise received by another who speaks not one's own tongue

cicatrix ex veritate: a bruise received for speaking one's mind openly *cicatrix ex silentio*: a bruise received for not speaking when one should

cicatrix ex mendacio: a bruise received for voicing untruths in an unconvincing fashion

cicatrix ex despoliatione: a bruise manifesting the legacy of attempted robbery

cicatrix audacia: a bruise received in battle (through bravery)

cicatrix ex pusillanimitate: a bruise received in battle (through cowardice)

cicatrix honesta: a bruise which enhances one's reputation

cicatrix viduatae: a bruise which exaggerates a melancholy beauty

cicatrix athletica: a bruise received while participating in athletic activity

cicatrix cygnis irati: a bruise inflicted by an angry swan

cicatrix experientiae prima: a bruise received as a direct result of experimentation

cicatrix experientiae secunda: a bruise received as an indirect result of experimentation

cicatrix penitus: a bruise received while tarrying inside a public building

cicatrix deforis: a bruise received while tarrying outside a public building

cicatrix crepusculo: a bruise inflicted at dusk

cicatrix ghibli: a bruise which blooms during the sirocco

cicatrix celsa: a bruise received at high altitudes

cicatrix sali: a bruise received on the high seas

BRUISES OF THE THIRD TYPE: MYSTERIOUS

cicatrix ex distractione: a bruise resulting from unthinking activity or distraction (not noticed at time of impact)

cicatrix somnambulatoris: a bruise acquired while sleep walking

cicatrix coelestis: a bruise inflicted by the will of God (most commonly through the mediation of an angel with special tools, as punishment for minor sins)

cicatrix lemuris: a bruise created through the mischief of spirits or jinns

cicatrix symbolica: a bruise which forms a sinister symbol, such as the Evil Eye

cicatrix lunaris: a bruise which waxes and wanes according to an unknown cycle

BRUISES OF THE FOURTH TYPE: INTERNAL/INVISIBLE

cicatrix sub praecordio: a bruise located beneath the rib cage stemming from grief

cicatrix in visceris: a bruise located in the pit of one's viscera from disappointment

cicatrix in gula: a bruise located in the throat from an unnamable fear

cicatrix in corde: a bruise located inside the heart from rejection by a beloved

cicatrix nigra: a bruise blossoming everblack from unrequited love (or requited love at a distance)

cicatrix cotidiana: a bruise created throughout the flesh by the daily pummeling of existence

APPENDIX III
MEMES

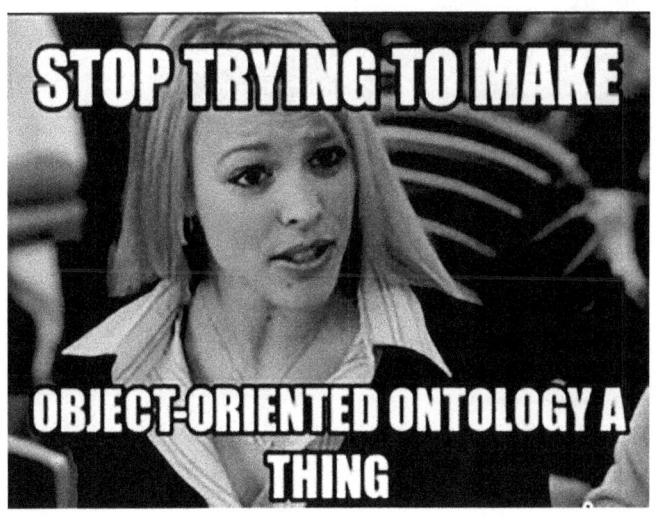

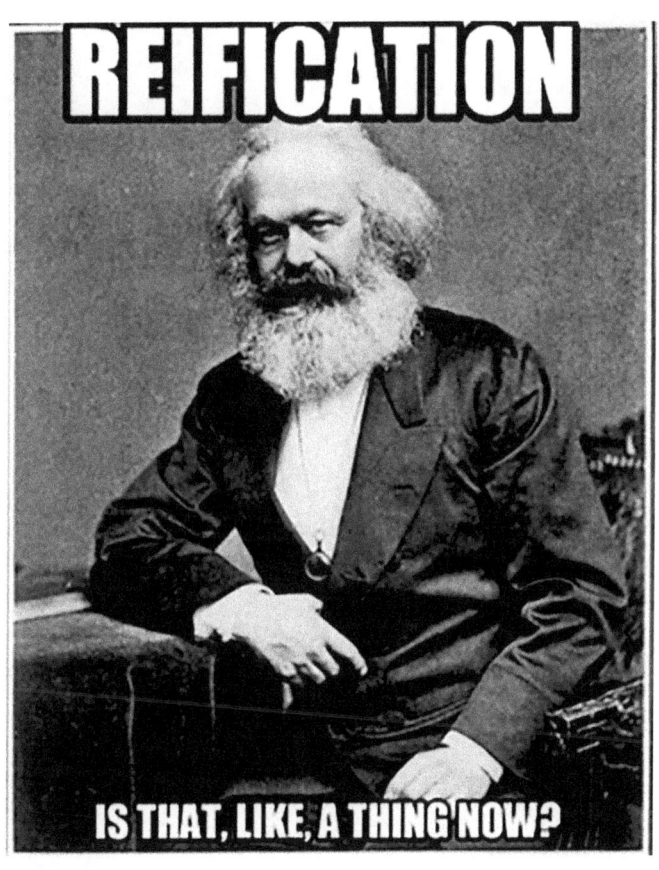

www.ingramcontent.com/pod-product-compliance
Lightning Source LLC
Chambersburg PA
CBHW060836190426
43197CB00040B/2640